NAVIGATION THE EASY WAY

NAVIGATION THE EASY WAY

☆ ☆ ☆ ☆ ☆ ☆ ☆

By

CARL D. LANE

AND

JOHN MONTGOMERY

W · W · NORTON & COMPANY · INC · *New York*

ISBN 0 393 03134 9
PRINTED IN THE UNITED STATES OF AMERICA
FOR THE PUBLISHERS BY THE VAIL-BALLOU PRESS, INC., BINGHAMTON, N. Y.
4 5 6 7 8 9

TO THE READER

THE authors of this book believe that anybody can navigate. There is no hocus-pocus about navigation; no magic formulas; no midnight wizardry. The only arithmetic required is simple, grade-school addition and subtraction—and not much of that.

This book presents the principles and practices of modern navigation in picture form, supplemented by text that any layman can understand. It starts with the simplest form of navigation and proceeds through piloting, dead reckoning and celestial navigation to an introduction to the electronic systems.

Primarily this book is intended to fix the principles of navigation firmly in the reader's mind. The authors know from experience that the stumbling block in learning navigation is failure to *see* the navigation picture through the dusty and obscure language of the astronomer and mathematician.

In this book we shall apply only the most necessary technical terms and take pains to explain and illustrate them simply. In addition there is a glossary at the end of the book in which the terms are explained again in everyday language.

Working out of celestial sights is done through the American Air Almanac and H.O.214, the most modern method in use today. As the American Nautical Almanac is being revised along the lines of the Air Almanac, knowledge of the Air Almanac will enable the reader to use both almanacs without further study. The revised Nautical Almanac will make its appearance in 1950, but we believe that the Air Almanac will remain the simpler and more convenient of the two and the easier for the beginner to understand.

This book will prove valuable to the sailor, the yachtsman, the aviator, to anyone studying for navigation examinations, and to the layman who has a general interest in the subject. We believe it will be of particular interest to those who have had difficulty in learning navigation by older methods or who have lost out for lack of mathematics.

The methods of demonstration used herein are based on practices employed during the last war in the U.S. Navy and the Army Air Corps when they were frequently faced with the task of teaching navigation in a hurry to men with no mathematical background and little or no sea or flight experience. The success of these methods is reflected in the enviable navigation record of the two organizations.

This book is made purposely small and light for easy reading in an arm chair or a bunk. It is not cluttered with complicated tables and technical diagrams. It does not demand constant reference to dictionaries and manuals. It is written in a continuous, step-by-step manner showing how all navigation is joined together by simple, common-sense ties.

It is navigation the easy way.

CARL D. LANE
JOHN MONTGOMERY

Camden, Maine
March, 1949.

EQUIPMENT

NOTHING more than this book is required for understanding the principles and methods of modern navigation. But for those who wish to follow the text with the navigation material used in the examples, the following should be obtained:

Coastal chart. A "1200" series of the area you know is recommended. Available at marine supply stores or from the Coast and Geodetic Survey, Washington. Price $0.75.

Protractor. Any type will do. Can be obtained from marine supply or school supply stores. Prices from $0.25 to $2.50.

Dividers. Obtainable at same places as above. Prices $0.25 to $2.00.

Parallel rulers. Obtainable at marine or draftsman's supply stores. Prices $1.00 to $2.50.

Air Almanac. Published for every four months of the year. Obtainable at marine or aviation supply stores or from the Superintendent of Documents, Washington, D.C. Price $1.50.

Tables of Computed Altitude and Azimuth (H.O.214). Published in one volume for every 10° of latitude. We suggest purchasing the volume covering your locality or the area you intend to navigate. Available at marine supply stores or from the Superintendent of Documents, Washington, D.C. Price $2.25 per volume.

THE essential purpose of navigation is getting from where you are to where you want to be. Every day you use navigation a thousand times—in crossing a room, in going to work, in walking or driving to market.

Walking across a field or meadow is very similar to crossing a body of water. You use a number of methods employed by navigators in guiding a ship across an ocean.

For instance—

One day you start to walk across a field from a pine tree to a poplar in the distance.

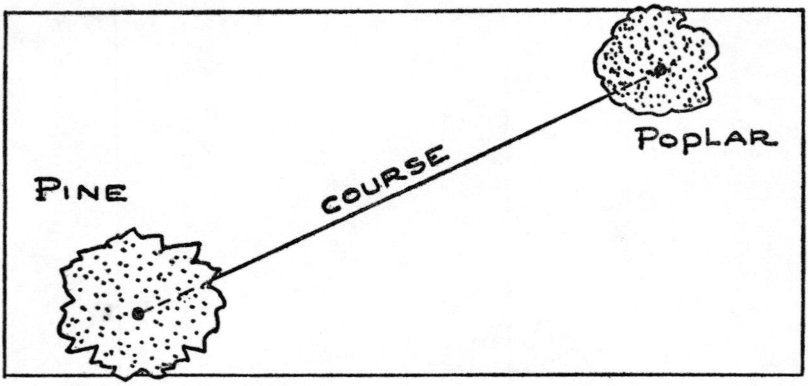

As long as the pine is directly behind you and the poplar directly in front of you there is no doubt but that you are on your course. You know that you are on a line that runs from the pine tree to the poplar. You do not know exactly at what point you are on that line unless you have something else to go by. But you *do* know you are on that line.

That line is highly important. It is called a *line of position* and is abbreviated LOP. It is the building brick of navigation and from the very beginning, where you are now, to the most advanced practices, you will be finding your way by laying down lines of position.

Now let us continue with our walk.

While you are on this line, still heading for the poplar, you discover at a certain instant that you are also directly between a windmill and an oak tree. Now halt your walk for a few seconds and take stock of what is happening to you.

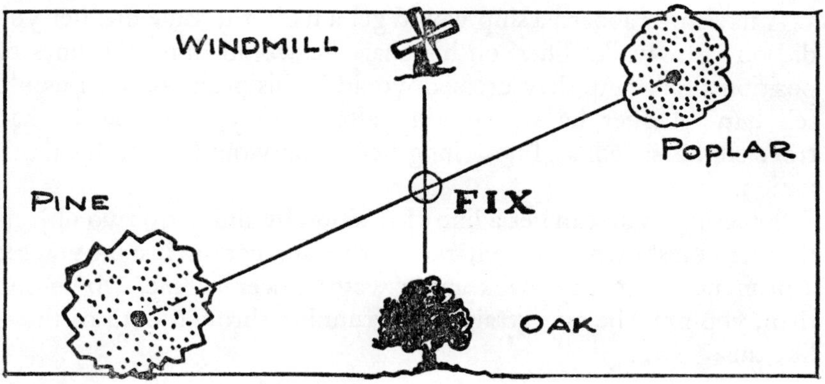

It is obvious that you now must be on *two* lines of position that cross or intersect at the very point where you are standing. This crossing or intersection is known as a *fix*, and the fix is where you are.

Now let's take this field to sea:

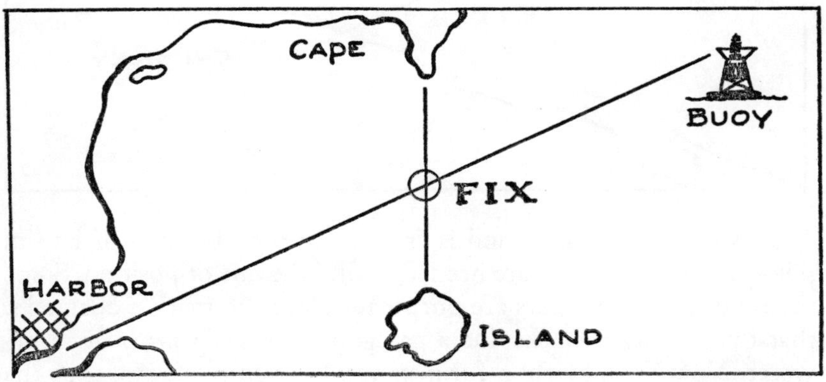

Here is the diagram at the top of the page translated into nautical language. The plan of the field has become a chart. The pine tree has become a harbor, the poplar a sea buoy, the windmill a cape, and the oak tree an island.

A navigator aboard a ship would get a fix in the same manner you did on your walk. Then on his chart he would draw the lines of position and where they crossed would be his position. This would tell him whether he was getting along safely, how far he had traveled, his speed, and how long before he would get to his destination.

Sometimes you can get a line of position by lining up two objects that are also shown on the chart. Say that at a certain instant you see a prominent chimney stack and a water tower in line. Obviously, then, you must be on a straight line running through both of them, like this:

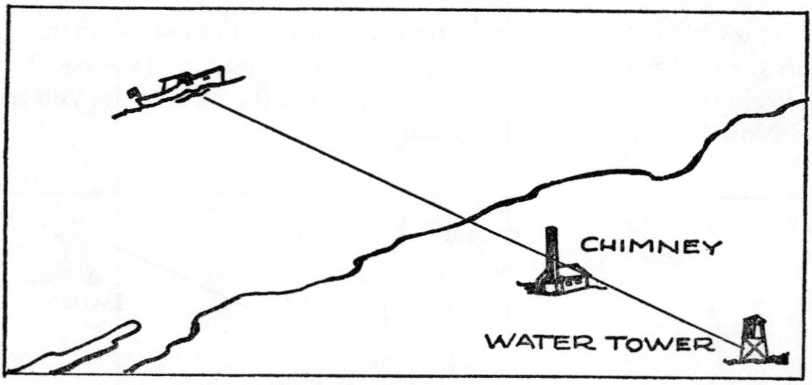

This is called a *range* and is frequently used because of its simplicity. No instruments are needed to find the line of position. Sometimes buoys and markers are purposely placed to mark a channel so that by keeping them in line a navigator can keep his boat in safe water. New York Harbor, for instance, has numerous ranges so that ships can navigate the narrow, twisting channels without danger.

Unfortunately, prominent landmarks are not often in convenient range and the navigator must rely on other means to determine his position. When he cannot find charted objects in range, or directly at his back and front, or on either side, he makes his compass work for him. A compass card looks like this:

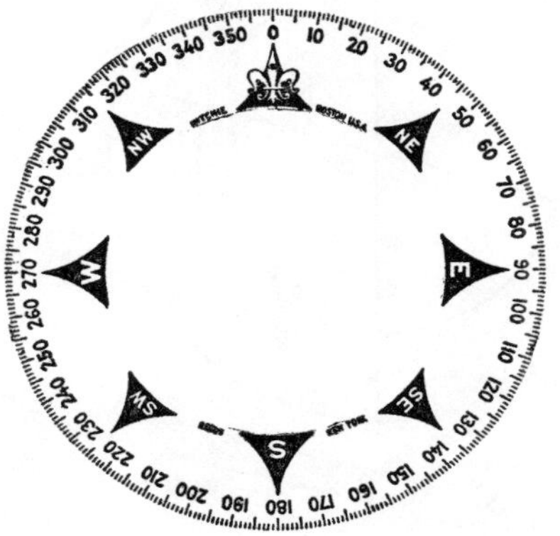

As you can see, a compass circle has 360° with North being 0°, East being 90°, South 180°, and West 270°.

Let us say you are sailing due north along the coast and see a lighthouse some distance off. You go to the compass, and sighting across the top of the card you see that it is bearing from you a certain number of degrees—say 75°.

If you look the other way across the compass card, you will see that directly opposite 75° is 255°. Therefore, if the lighthouse is bearing 75° from you, you in turn must be bearing 255° from it.

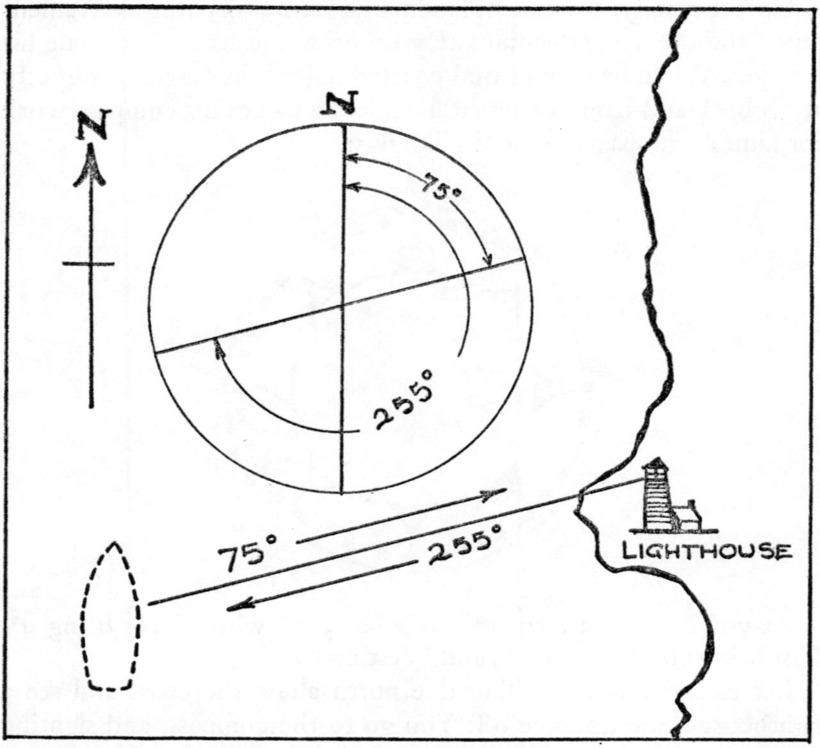

You don't know where *you* are. But you do know where the lighthouse is because it is printed in its *exact* position on the chart. So you draw a line on the chart using a *protractor* (which is a compass circle or part of one and is the same little piece of celluloid you used in geometry in school). You start the line at the lighthouse and draw it straight at an angle of 255° from North.

That is your line of position.

You are somewhere on that line.

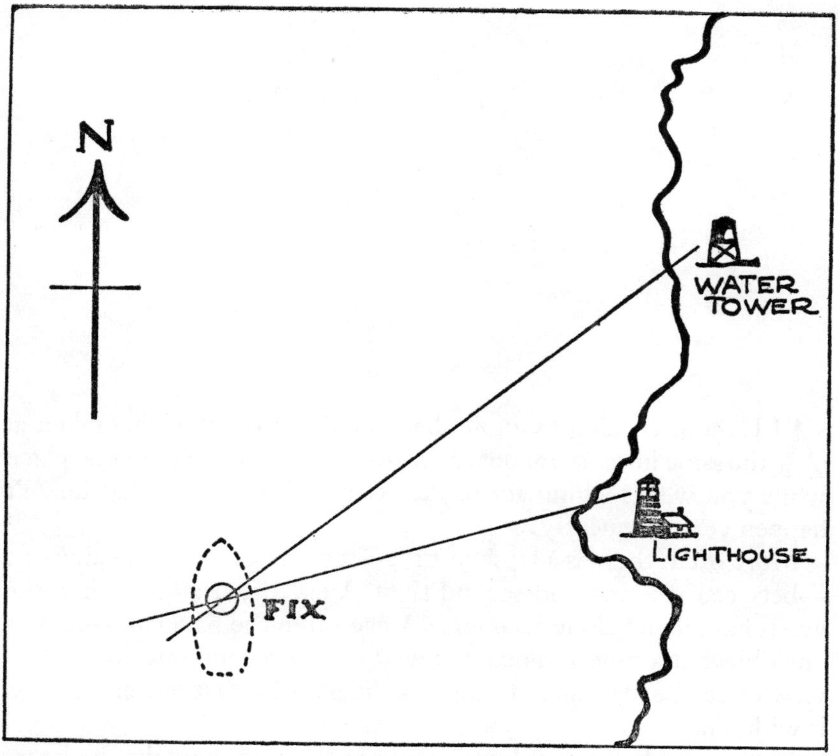

At the same time you take a similar sight on another prominent object along the coast. Let us say this time you find a water tower further along the shore line.

You repeat the same process as with the lighthouse.

Where the lines cross is your fix.

That is where you are.

ALL the preceding examples have had to do with sights taken at the same instant, or aboard a vessel that stayed in the same place while you were looking across the compass. Obviously that doesn't happen very frequently.

More often there is a lapse of time—sometimes a considerable one—between the first and second sight. Very often all this time the vessel has moved along its course. Very often the navigator sees but one object at a time and he must wait until a second one comes into view or can be identified. In this case he plots his first line and carries it with him.

Let us say a half hour elapses between the time you take the lighthouse sight and the water-tower sight. You estimate from the speed of the boat the distance you have traveled in half an hour.

You measure the distance on the course line from the exact point where the lighthouse line crossed the course and draw a line exactly parallel to the lighthouse line. This is known as your *advanced* lighthouse line. It would look like this after the water-tower line had also been plotted:

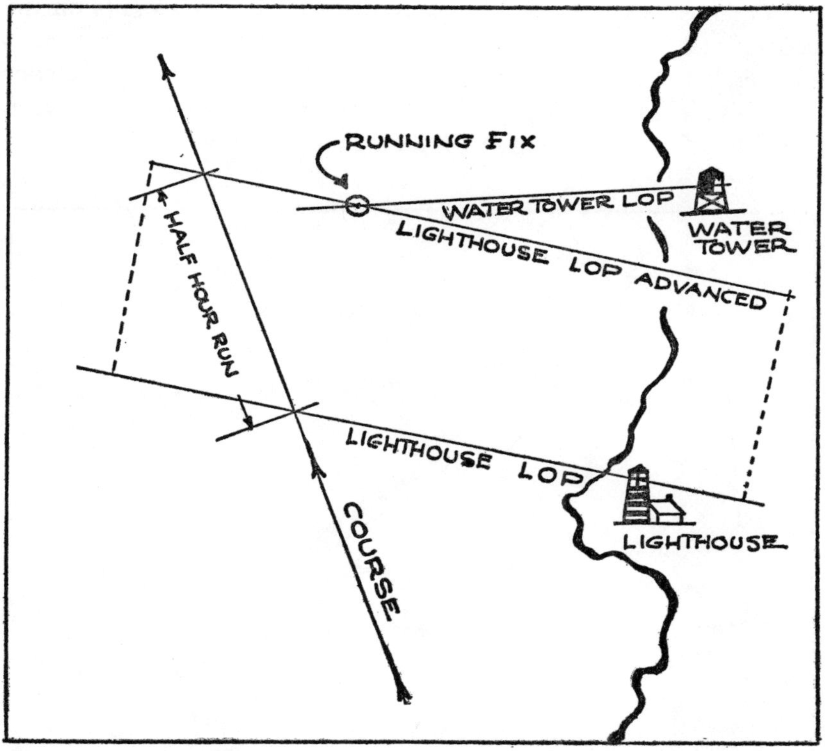

Where the advanced lighthouse line crosses the water-tower line is your *running* fix. (Note that the fix shows you to be considerably off your course.)

Naturally this kind of fix is not as accurate as an instantaneous fix. There will be a probable error in estimating speed and there will be some drift of the boat due to wind or current. But running fixes, because of necessity, are the most frequently used. Later on you will see how the navigator will advance a line of position for several hours to obtain a running fix. For if a ship is held on her course and the speed and drift accurately estimated, a running fix will be as reliable as any other.

Sometimes a navigator plots a running fix by two sights on the same object. The same method is used except that enough time is allowed between the two sights to permit the angles to change considerably. This gives a good *cut,* for the wider the angle between two lines of position the more accurate the fix is apt to be.

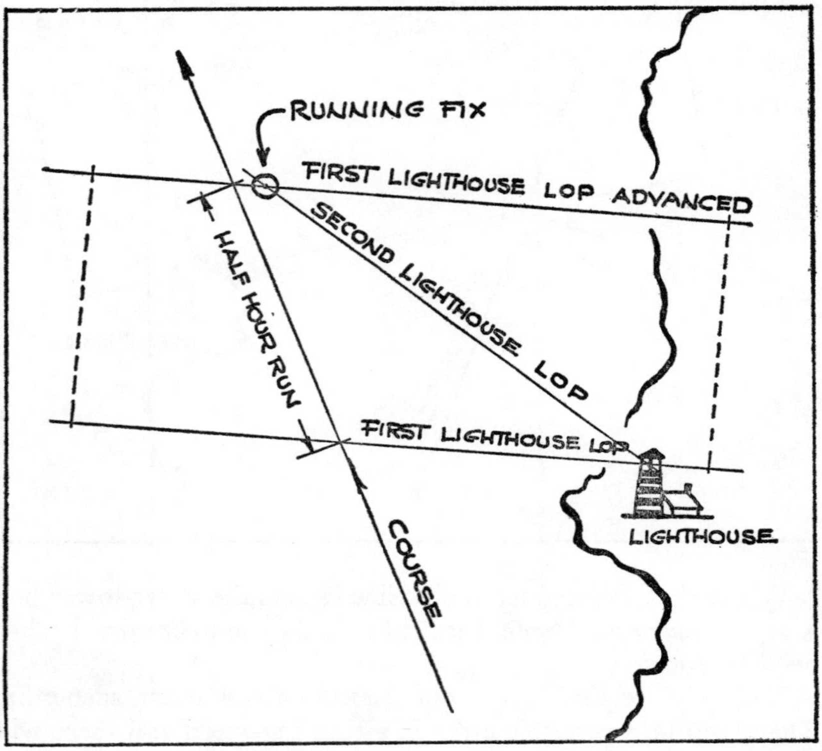

This is a valuable method when far off the course or during poor visibility when only one object can be seen and identified. Often the single sight is advanced several times to determine possible error in estimating drift and speed.

In proceeding along the course it is necessary for the navigator always to know how far offshore he is. Reefs and other hidden dangers usually dot the coast line. There are numerous methods of determining offshore distance, but here is the simplest and most popular way:

Take a sight when a known object bears exactly 45° from the boat—not 45° from true North as we have done before, but 45° from the bow of the boat or the direction it is heading. Check the time and the boat speed and keep watching the object. When it bears 90°, or when you are even or abeam with it, check your time again. Figure out the distance you have traveled during this period.

That distance is the distance you are from the object.

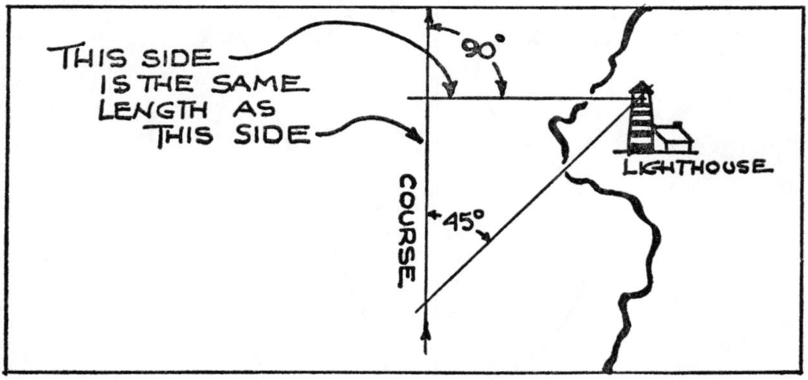

In simple geometry what you have done is to measure one side of an isoceles triangle. The other side must be the same length.

This is known as the *bow and beam bearing;* it is very popular with fishermen and others not carrying navigation equipment.

Sometimes it is necessary to know the distance off you *will* be if you keep steering the same course.

This time you start when the object bears 22½° from the bow. You keep time as you did before and measure your distance when the object bears 45°.

The distance off you will be when abeam of the object is 7/10 of the distance covered from 22½° to 45°.

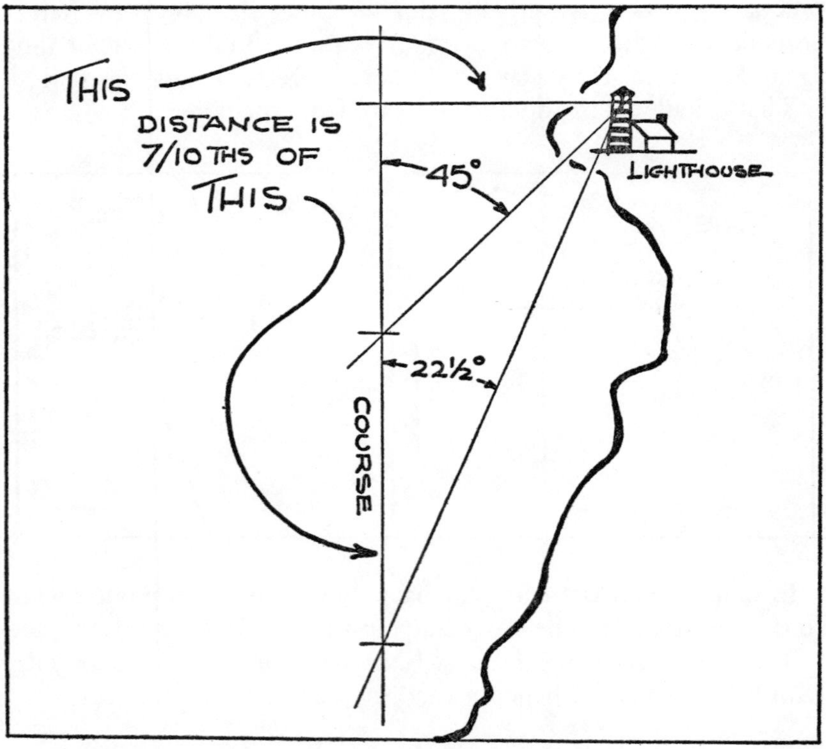

This is known as *doubling the angle on the bow* and is valuable when wind or current is apt to carry you too close inshore.

A CHART is similar to a map except that a chart is concerned with the water and its dangers and only those landmarks that can be used by the navigator.

A chart is a small section of the globe flattened out. The most frequently used method of flattening out is called the *Mercator Projection* and it is the only one we will consider. All coastal charts and most deep-sea charts are Mercator charts.

Charts are published by the Federal government and can be obtained from it or from ship supply stores or stationers in coastal towns. They cost less than a dollar apiece. It would be a good idea to have one handy as you read this and subsequent pages. A "1200" series of the coast line you are familiar with would be the best. This series costs $0.75 a chart.

On the next page we reprint a portion of Chart 1211 showing the southern shore of Connecticut, Fishers Island, and the Race, the body of water that connects Long Island Sound with Block Island Sound.

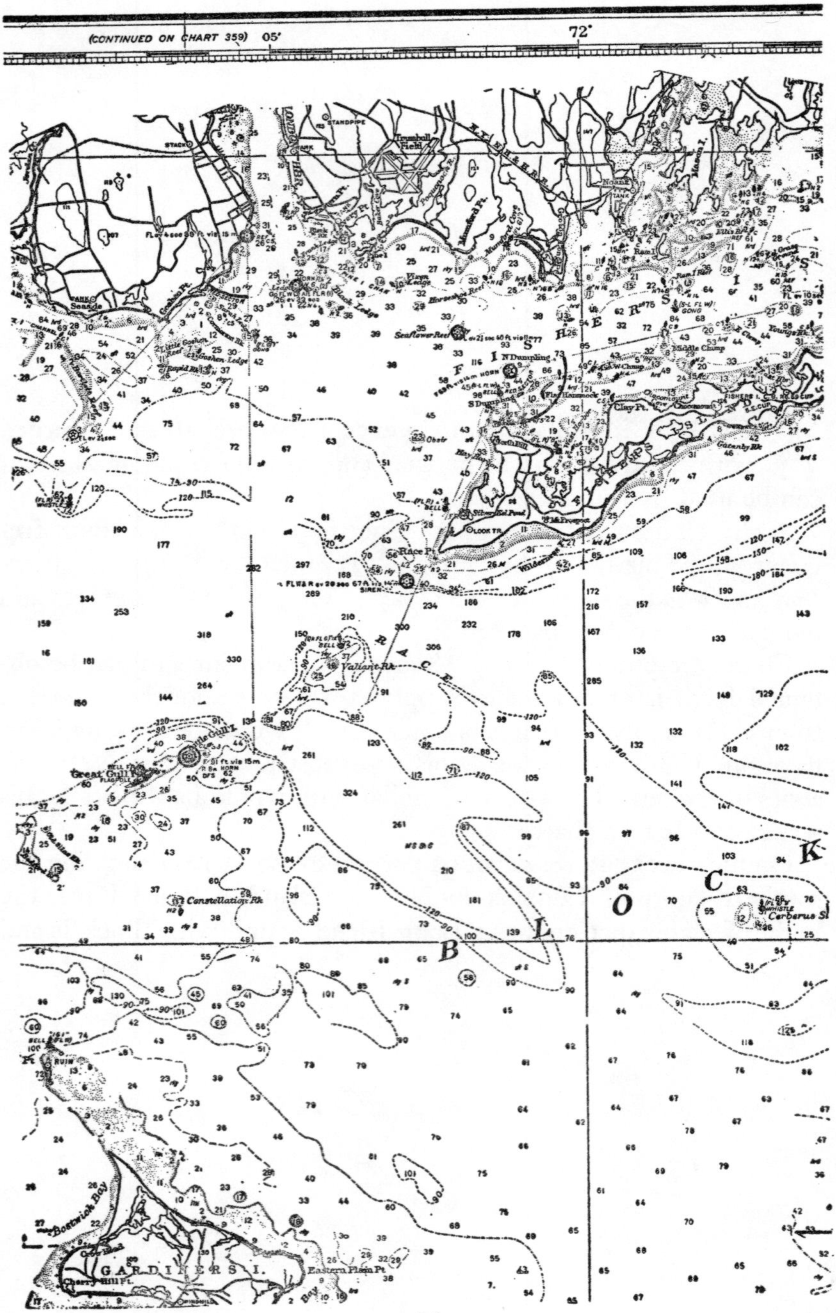
(CONTINUED ON CHART 359)
05'
72°
Trumbull Field
STANDPIPE
STACK
Seaside
Race Pt.
Valiant Rk.
Great Gull I.
Constellation Rk.
Bostwick Bay
GARDINERS I.
Eastern Plain Pt.
Cherry Hill Pt.
Flat Hammock
Clay Pt.
Gatenby Rk.
Cerberus S.
Seaflower Reef
Horseshoe Reef
N Dumpling
S Dumpling
Noank
Ram I.
Mason I.
FISHERS I.
SIREN
LOOK TR.
RUIN
BLOCK
RACE
FISHERS
ISLAND

Because of limitation of space, no effort will be made here to explain the abbreviations and symbols used in charts. Most of them are self-explanatory. The reader is recommended to purchase from a marine supply store the government publication "Chart Symbols and Abbreviations" ($0.10) for detailed explanation.

In selecting a chart the prudent navigator makes certain of the following:

1. It is up-to-date. Charts are corrected frequently to follow changes in the buoyage system, soundings, lights, etc.

2. It covers the area wanted with plenty of room to spare.

3. It is of sufficiently large scale. Some dangers will not appear in a large-area small-scale chart. For instance the chart on the opposite page is too small a scale to be used in entering Fishers Island Sound or the Thames River. Chart 359, a harbor chart, should be used instead.

DISTANCE at sea, both on the surface of the water, under it, and above it, is not measured by the land mile, which is only common to the United States and the British Commonwealth, but is measured by the nautical or sea mile which is common to the whole world. The nautical mile is about one-seventh longer than the land mile and is an exact segment of the circle of the earth. On a Mercator chart it is the same as one minute of latitude.

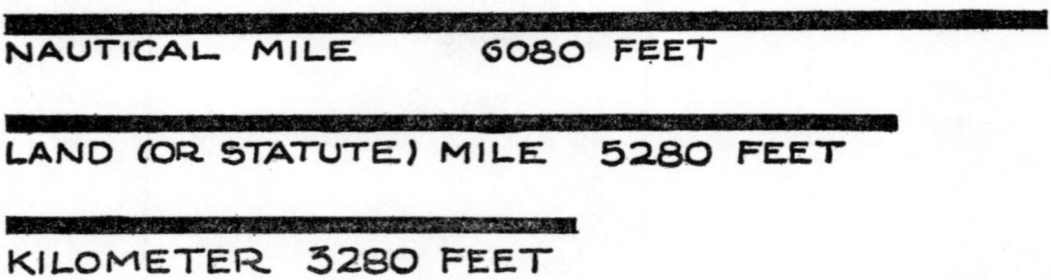

Distance is measured by land or sea markings, by bearings or sights, or by estimation or reckoning. This latter method is called *dead reckoning*, a corruption of the old-fashioned term, "deduced reckoning."

As you can see, dead reckoning is based upon a knowledge of the speed of the vessel. For that reason the navigator always knows the speed he is traveling.

In motor-driven vessels, from motorboats to ocean liners, the speed is estimated by the revolutions of the engine. Every large vessel has a table made up by the builder of the ship showing the speed at various engine turnings. In small boats and yachts the owner has determined the speed of his boat at various readings of the *R.P.M.* (*Revolutions per Minute*) *indicator* by numerous runs in still water.

RPM INDICATOR

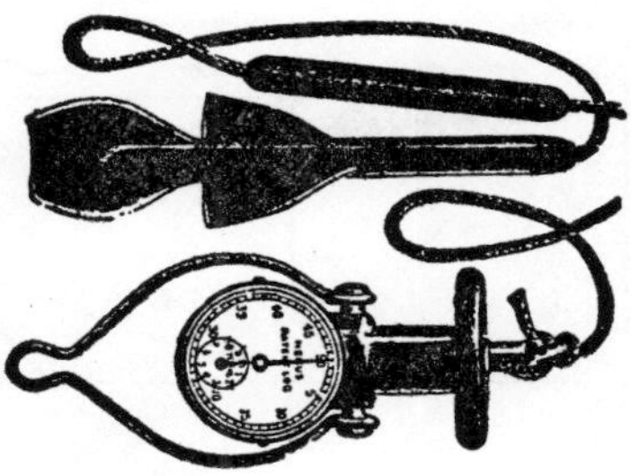

TAFF RAIL LOG

In sailboats speed is determined by a *taffrail log*. This is a dial attached to a propeller on the end of a cable that is streamed out from the stern of the vessel. The propeller and cable, revolving as the boat moves through the water, slowly move the dial. The reading is similar to the mileage dial of the automobile speedometer. Taffrail logs are frequently used by motor vessels to check the R.P.M. indicator.

Nautical speed is calculated by so many nautical miles per hour, or *knots*. A boat making 12 knots will cover 12 nautical miles in an hour's time.

Distance on a Mercator chart is found by the scale in the corner of the chart or by the intermittent black and white bars on each side (not top or bottom). As there may be a slight difference in the length of these bars from the top to the bottom of the chart it is important that you measure the side bars as close to your course line as possible.

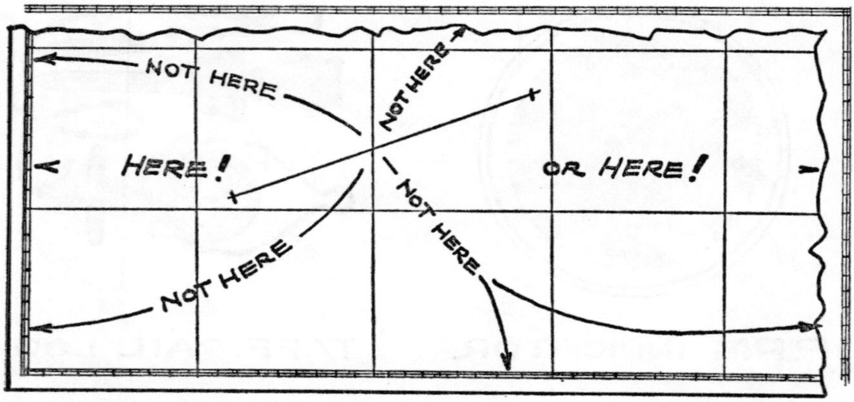

THE basic instruments for chart work are:

Protractor
Dividers
Parallel Rulers

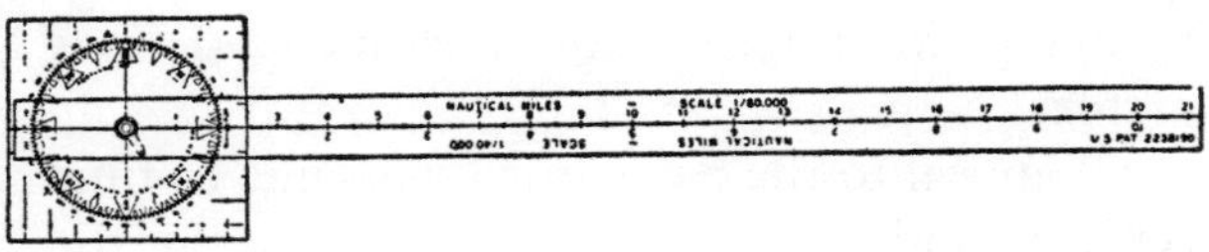

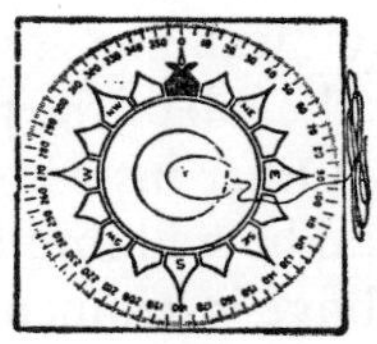

PROTRACTORS

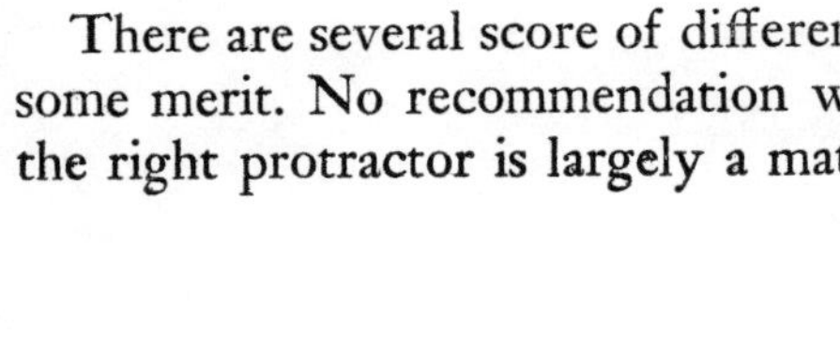

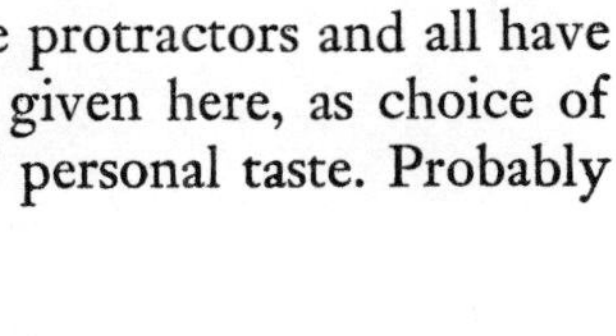

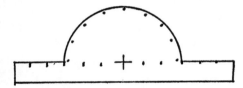

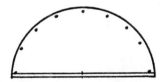

There are several score of different type protractors and all have some merit. No recommendation will be given here, as choice of the right protractor is largely a matter of personal taste. Probably the most popular type for coastal work is the single arm protractor (sometimes called the *course protractor*) which combines a 360° circle with a straight edge.

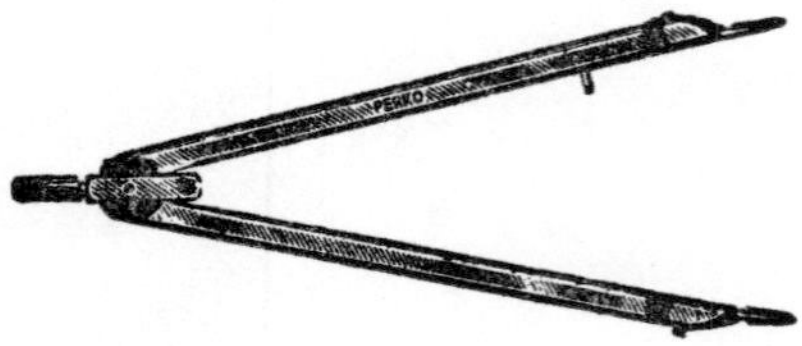

Basically a protractor is merely an instrument for measuring an angle. It is used in laying down courses and plotting lines of position by leveling its base on lines of latitude or longitude or the printed border of the chart.

Dividers are for measuring distance, using the scale or the latitude bars for a standard.

Parallel rulers are used for advancing lines of position evenly. The old-fashioned use of parallel rulers to determine courses or bearings by "walking" them from a compass rose is not recommended. This is the job of the protractor.

Other instruments will appeal to the navigator from time to time and he will find convenience and pleasure in many of them. But the above instruments are all that are needed for chart work in modern navigation.

In using the simple, semi-circular protractor, which is generally made of celluloid, the bottom or base is lined up with a line of latitude, or the east-west black lines that cross the chart, and the angle of the course or line of position read off from the figures stamped on the edge.

On northbound courses the protractor is placed so that the rounded top is north; on southbound courses the proctractor is placed upside down. Some difficulty may be encountered on some protractors, depending on where the zero or beginning is stamped. A little thought, however, should untangle this problem as the protractor is a segment of a circle, and every circle has 360°.

This slight difficulty is done away with in the single arm or course protractor which is a complete circle and gives the course from one position. The arm or straight edge is placed parallel with the course line and the protractor rotated until it is in line with a line of latitude or longitude. The arm cuts the protractor circle at the true angle.

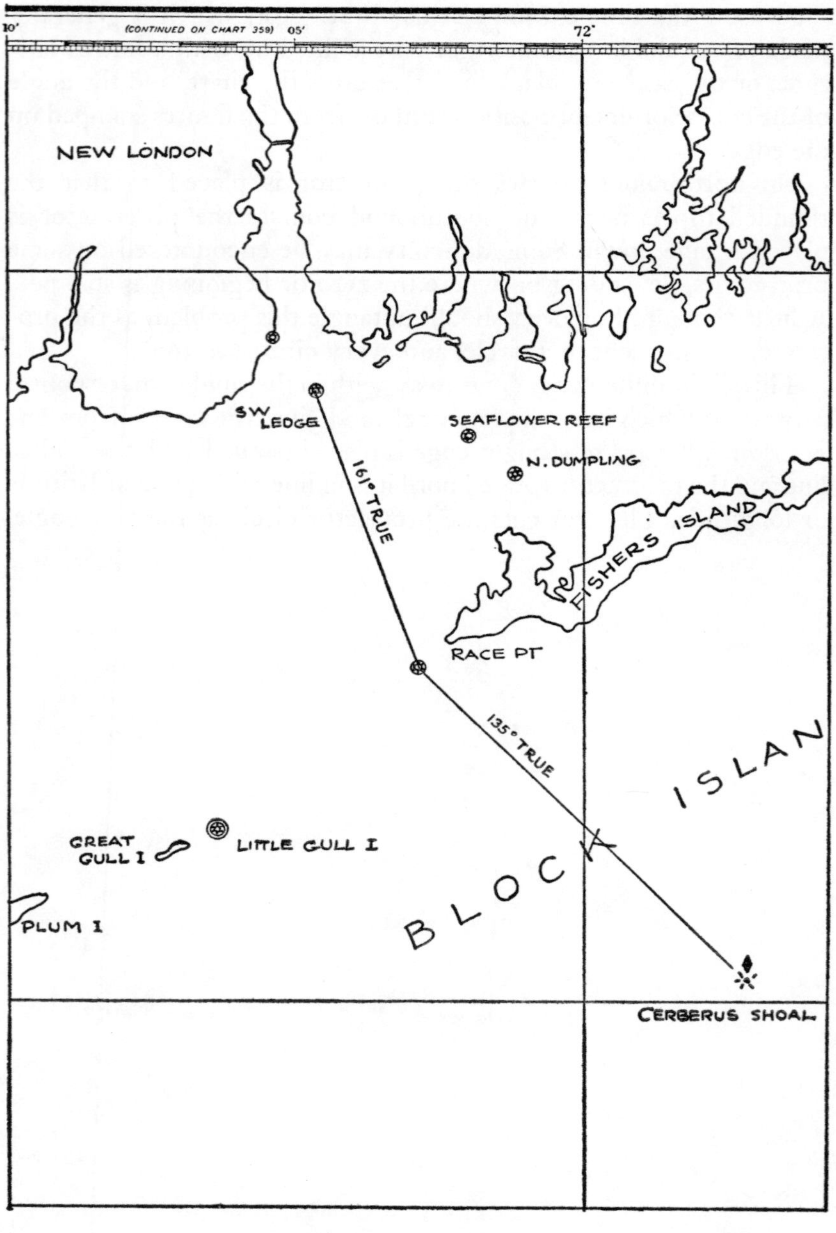
10'
(CONTINUED ON CHART 359)
05'
72°
NEW LONDON
SW LEDGE
SEAFLOWER REEF
N. DUMPLING
161° TRUE
FISHERS ISLAND
RACE PT
135° TRUE
BLOCK ISLAN
GREAT GULL I
LITTLE GULL I
PLUM I
CERBERUS SHOAL

Let us follow a navigator as he plots a course from New London to Cerberus Shoal. (This is the same area that is covered in the printed portion of Chart 1211.)

After following the channel out of New London harbor and down the Thames River he takes his departure from Southwest Ledge Light.

Because of the interference of Fishers Island he cannot sail direct to Cerberus Shoal but must go through The Race. He takes a ruler or straight edge and draws a line on the chart from Southwest Ledge Light to Race Point Light. Next he takes his protractor and finds the true course to be 161°.

From Race Point Light he plots a line to Cerberus Shoal Light. His protractor tells him that the true course is 135°.

In other words, he must steer to make good a course of 161° to Race Point Light, thence a course of 135° to Cerberus Shoal Light.

Taking his dividers, he measures off the distance he must travel on each leg and estimates by the boat's rated speed when he should be at each point. This is known as the *Estimated Time of Arrival* or *ETA;* it is highly important to know in case he is suddenly blinded by fog.

The lines are now labeled with the true course angle and the distance, and the points are marked with the *ETA*.

THE compass has always been, and doubtless always will be, the navigator's chief tool. While there are many new types of compasses, operating on various principles, the simple magnetic compass is the standard instrument and generally the most trustworthy.

The magnetic compass operates by the attraction of a magnetized needle to the magnetic poles, which are close by the true North and South Poles. In a marine compass the needle is attached to a round card upon which is printed the 360° circle. This is floated in a bowl of liquid.

On the inside of the bowl is engraved a hairline that is directly in line with the bow of the boat. The mariner heads his boat in the direction he wants to go by turning his steering wheel or tiller until the degree of his course is on the same degree mark of the card. He keeps on his course by keeping that degree mark on the hairline.

This hairline is known as the *lubber's line.*

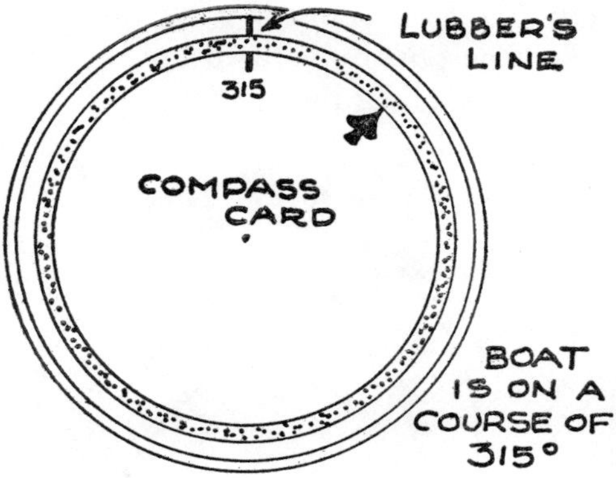

The magnetic compass is subject to two errors, both of which must be corrected for before the course can be correctly or safely steered.

First is what is termed *variation.* This is caused by the fact that the true North Pole and the Magnetic North Pole are not in the same place. (The same is true of the true South Pole and the Magnetic South Pole. But for reasons of simplicity we will talk only of the North Poles.)

The top of the world looks something like this:

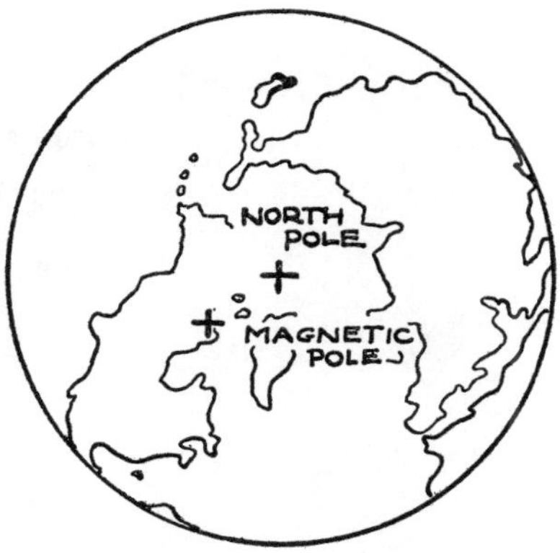

It is obvious that if the compass points to the magnetic pole, then it points to the true pole only when the two are in line—which is not often the case. Look at this diagram:

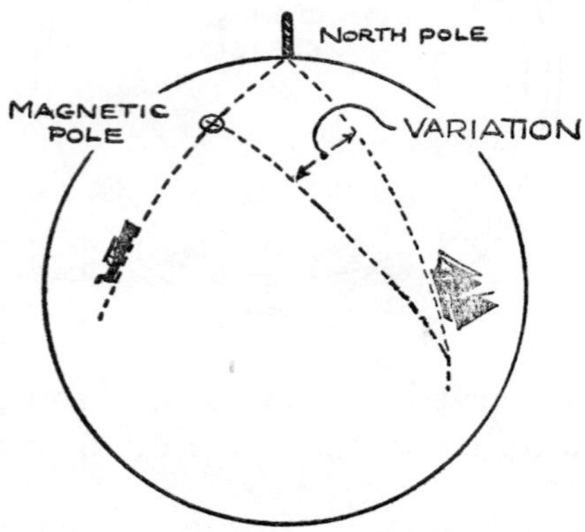

The ship on the left has the magnetic pole in line with the North Pole. Therefore, there is no variation in this case. The ship on the right does not have the magnetic pole in line with the North Pole; therefore its compass does not point to true North. The difference between the direction of the two poles is *variation,* which the navigator must correct for by adding or subtracting the difference from his true course.

Variation for every locality is found on the chart. On charts of very large areas the lines of variation are printed across the face. On all charts, however, variation can be found by the compass *rose,* several of which are printed on each chart, which gives a graphic picture of the variation as well as telling whether it is east or west and what the annual change of variation will be, if any.

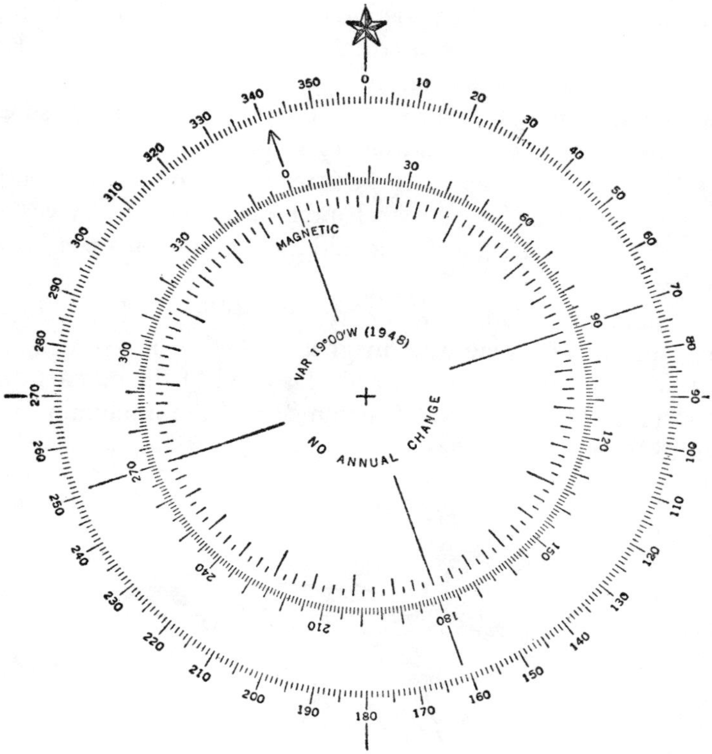

If you found the above compass rose on your chart you would know that the variation is 19° to the west of true North. The inner circle shows the direction of the magnetic pole; the outer circle the direction of the true pole. Therefore, to steer a true course you must *add* 19° to your compass heading. If you wanted to make good a true course of 40°, you must steer a course of 40° plus 19°, or 59°. If you wanted to make good a course of 190°, you must steer 190° plus 19°, or 209°.

On the other hand, if the variation is *east*, that is, if the arrow of the inner circle is pointing *east* of true North, then the variation is *subtracted* from your true course.

The second compass error is called *deviation* and is not so easily discovered, as it differs aboard every ship.

While the compass seems to be interested only in the magnetic pole it is also tempted by iron, steel and nickel, and as every vessel has some such metal aboard, it can be said that all compasses suffer from some deviation.

You can understand deviation readily if you will consider the compass needle as a very light magnet—which it is—and the metal near it as being very heavy or firmly fastened. If the magnet cannot draw the metal to it, it, like Mohammed and the mountain, will be drawn to the metal.

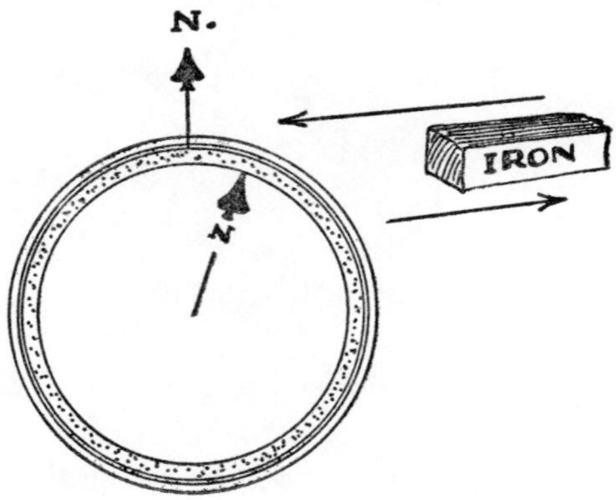

As the amount of this error will depend upon the nearness and location of the metal, the only way to determine it properly is to have an expert prepare a list of deviation—called a deviation card—for the principal points of the compass. This is the method used in large ships.

In smaller boats and yachts the owner should find his deviation on several headings and have his compass *compensated*. This is the installation of iron bars in certain positions around the compass that will offset the deviation forces by luring the needle back to its proper position.

If a compass is not compensated, then the navigator must use a deviation card. The most popular form is one like this:

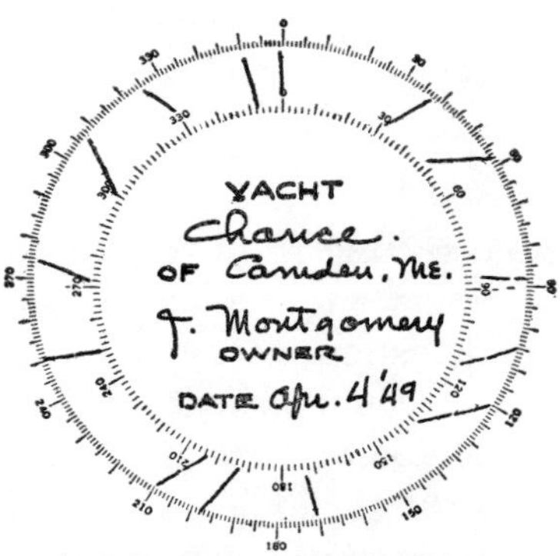

YACHT
Chance.
OF Camden, Me.
J. Montgomery
OWNER
DATE Apr. 4 '49

A DEVIATION CARD

Deviation, like variation, is marked east and west and its correction is made in the same manner. When a true course is corrected for variation and deviation it is called a *compass course* and is the course given the steersman.

There are many memory joggers and jingles for applying compass corrections, but none is necessary if you study the compass rose for a few seconds. However, for those who want to by-pass this effort, one of the simplest and easiest-to-remember joggers is this:

THIN
TRUE

COWS
COMPASS

SELDOM
SUBTRACT

EAT
EAST

In other words, in correcting from true to compass courses you must subtract east variation and deviation. Naturally you would add west variation and deviation.

In general practice it is common to combine the two errors for a net error. For instance where there is 12° east variation and 5° west deviation, the net error would be 7° East, which would be subtracted from the true course for the compass course.

ON any chart you will see several black lines that crisscross the sheet and end in the margins where they are marked by numbered degrees (°) and minutes (′), or one-sixtieth of degrees.

These are the lines of *latitude* and *longitude* and they are the streets and avenues of the navigator and geographer. The lines or *parallels* of latitude run east and west and the lines or *meridians* of longitude run north and south. Knowing the latitude and longitude of a place, we can spot it exactly on a map or a globe. To say a place is 34 21 N and 81 22 W is like saying that a place is on the corner of Poplar Avenue and Hemlock Street.

Here is the way latitude and longitude are marked on a map of the United States:

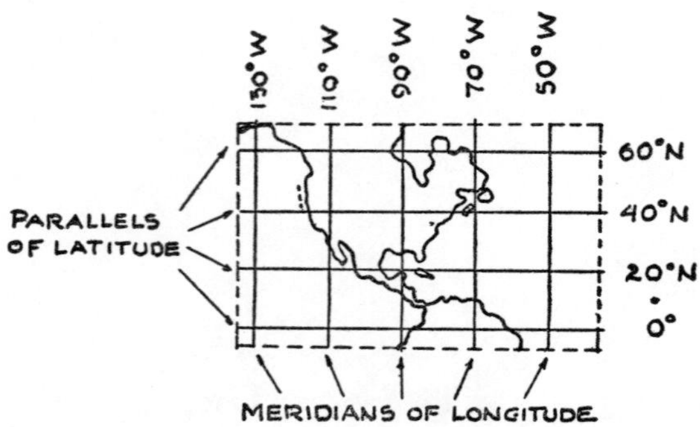

Here is the same map in its place on the globe:

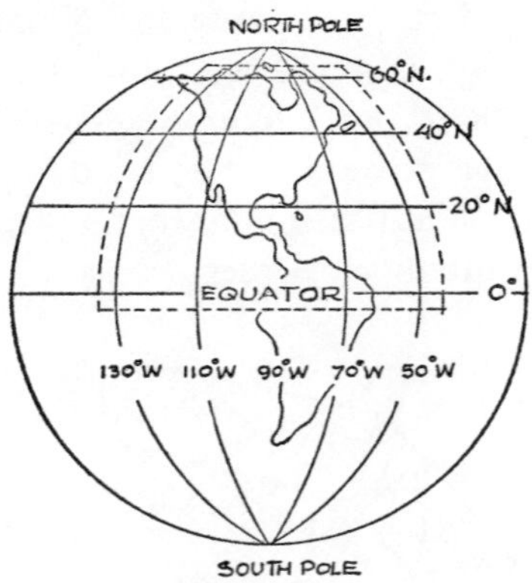

Note that the parallels of latitude on the map are just part of lines that run east and west around the globe, and that the meridians on the map are part of the lines that run from pole to pole.

Let us think about the earth as an orange. The top of the orange where it joins the branch is the North Pole, and the bottom speck is the South Pole.

Around the middle of the orange, exactly half way between the North Pole and the South Pole, is the *equator.*

Now latitude on the earth is simply the distance north or south of the equator. All lines of latitude run horizontally around the earth exactly *parallel* to the equator, hence their name *parallels.*

The distance is measured in degrees and minutes. As every circle has 360°, you can see by looking at your orange that the distance from the equator to the North Pole is one fourth of a circle, or 90°. Therefore, the North Pole in latitude is 90° North, or simply 90N.

The city of Washington is on a parallel of latitude that is 38° and 55′ north of the equator; therefore, its latitude is 38 55N. The city of Rio de Janeiro is on a parallel of latitude that is 22° and 54′ south of the equator, hence its latitude is 22 54S. Any other spot marked 38 55N is directly east or west of Washington, and any other spot marked 22 54S is directly east or west of Rio.

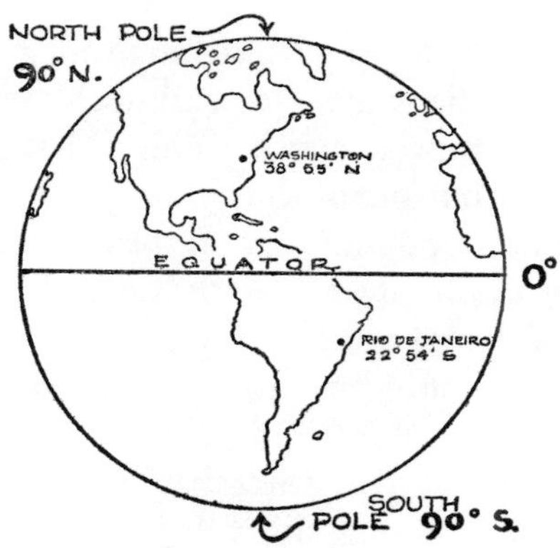

Now to discuss longitude we must unpeel the orange.

See how the segment lines run from the North Pole to the South Pole.

These are the lines or meridians of longitude.

Note how the meridians are closer and closer together as they leave the equator and approach either pole. That is why we use the side and not the top or bottom of the chart to measure by. If you will look at your 1200 chart you will see that the minutes of longitude are much smaller than the minutes of latitude and are, therefore, unreliable for measuring mileage distance.

Longitude is also measured in degrees and minutes, but from east to west or from west to east. All measurements start from the zero meridian which is the one that runs through Greenwich, a suburb of London. Hence it is commonly called the *Greenwich Meridian*, or just *Greenwich.*

Longitude is measured west to the 180° meridian or east to the same meridian.

Here is a diagram of longitude looking at the earth from below the

South Pole, or if you were at the South Pole and looking north:

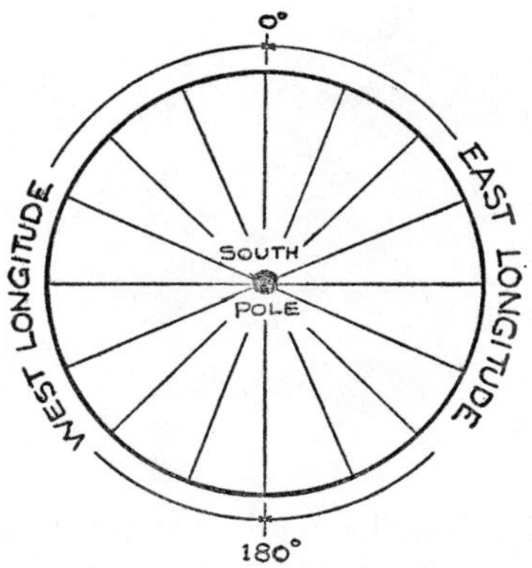

Washington being 77 04W, Rio de Janeiro being 43 13W, and Bombay being 72 49E means that they are on meridians that are that far east and west of Greenwich.

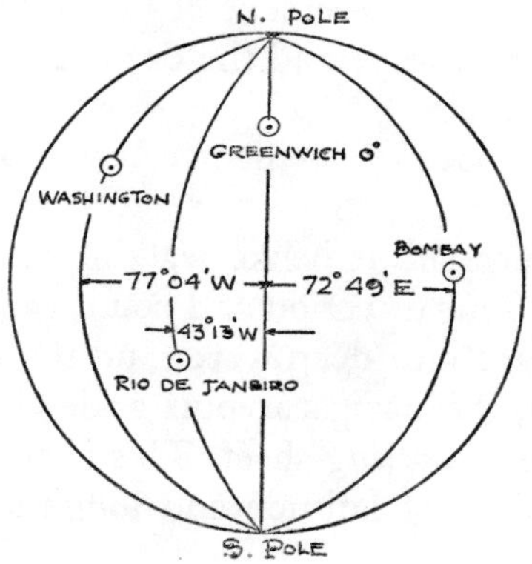

Think of latitude and longitude as being lines of position. If a place is 43 24N, it is on a line of position running east and west 43° and 24′ north of the equator. If its longitude is 91 06W, it is on a line of position running north and south 91° and 6′ west of Greenwich. Where those lines cross is that place's fix.

IN offshore navigation the navigator must rely heavily on dead reckoning. He must keep accurate track of the ship's movement and be able to estimate instantly the ship's position at any given moment. Any changes of course or speed are entered at once in his *logbook* (which is his daily record), and on the chart.

Naturally, without checks of some sort a ship can get considerably off course after many hours or several days of dead reckoning, but sometimes there is no escape and the dead-reckoning position is all the navigator can obtain.

On the whole, dead reckoning demands no more than very careful plotting on the part of the navigator and very careful steering on the part of the steersman. It is like walking in the dark when you must be certain of your direction and count each footstep.

When a ship heads into deep water and the coast is no longer a matter of concern, the navigator puts aside the regular chart and plots his course on a *plotting* sheet. This is similar to a chart, but blank except for lines of latitude and longitude and the compass roses. Plotting sheets are published by the government and sold directly or through marine supply stores at a cost of $0.10 to $0.30 a sheet, depending on the size and style. They are printed for every few degrees of latitude, and the navigator must be sure to use the sheet covering his area.

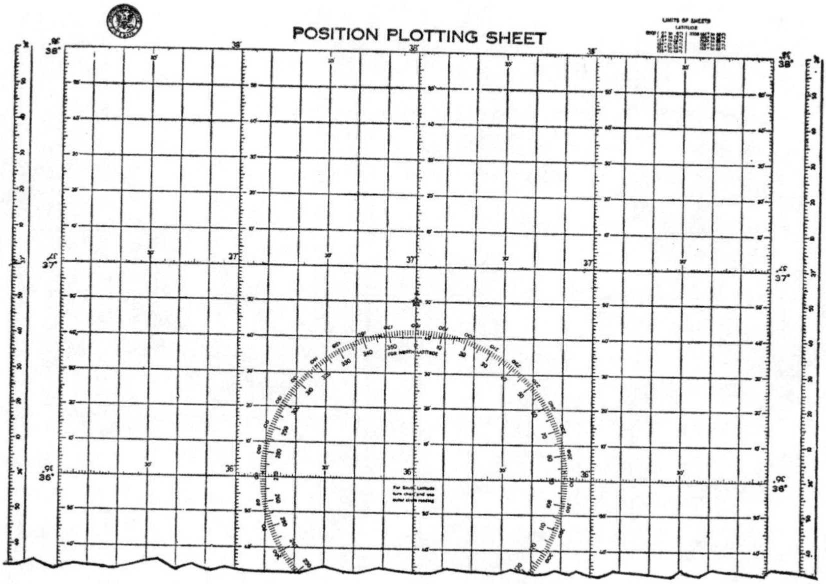

Many navigators use plotting sheets at all times in plotting bearings, radio and celestial fixes, etc., transferring only the fixes to the chart itself. This keeps the chart cleaner and less crowded.

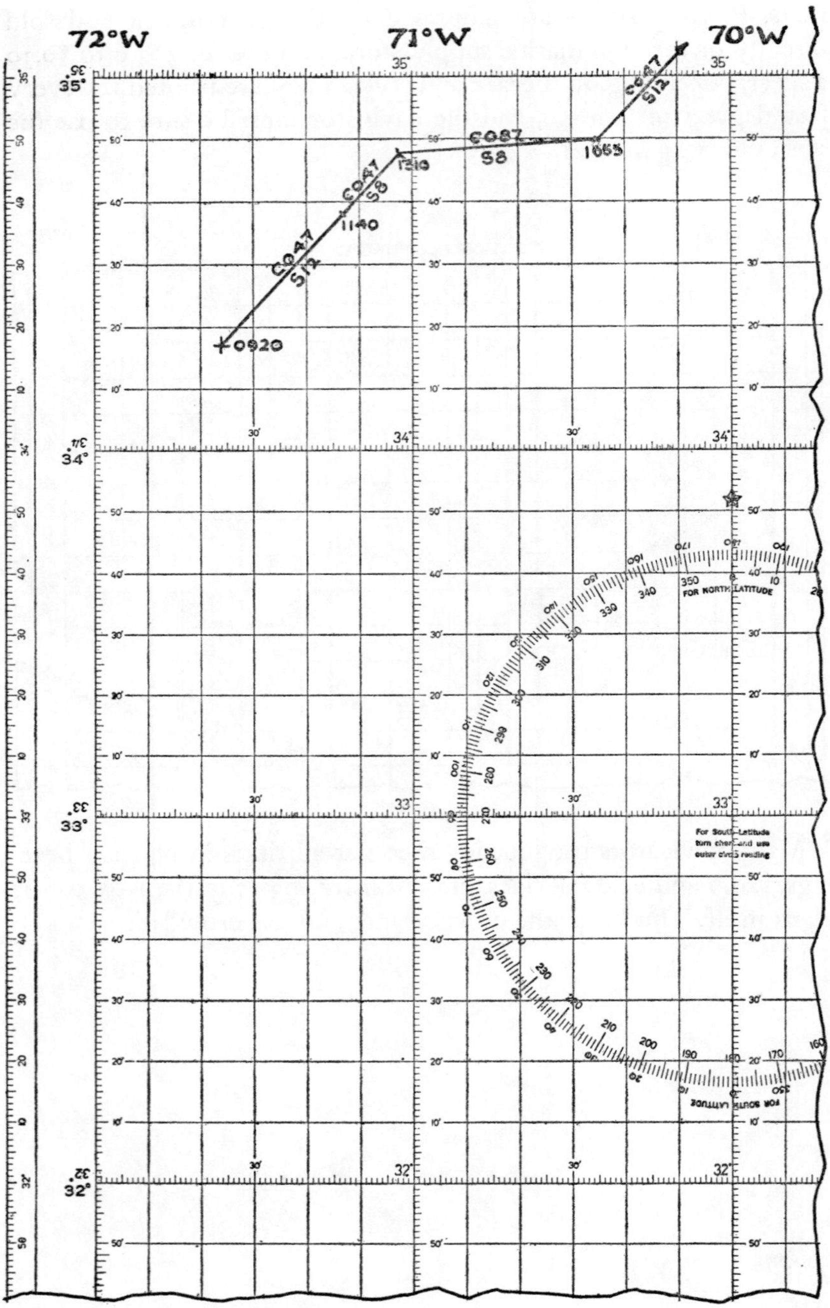
72°W
71°W
70°W
C047
S12
C047
S8
1140
1310
C087
S8
1053
C047
S12
0920
FOR NORTH LATITUDE
For South Latitude turn chart and use outer circle reading
FOR SOUTH LATITUDE

Because of the importance of knowing the position at all times, the navigator customarily calculates the distance traveled and marks the dead-reckoning position on the course line each hour. Close inshore or in doubtful water the position is marked every half hour. The course line is also marked whenever the speed is changed, and naturally a new course line is laid down if the heading is changed.

Let us take a look at the plotting sheet of a navigator aboard a ship enroute from Savannah to Liverpool. Below is his log and to the left is the plotting sheet.

0920 Celestial fix gives position at 34 17N, 71 36W. Course 47° true. Speed 12 knots.
1140 Rain squalls and poor visibility. Speed reduced to 8 knots.
1310 Heavy seas over bow. Course changed to 87° true.
1655 Seas quieting. Course resumed of 47° true. Speed increased to 12 knots. Dead-reckoning position, 34 50N, 70 25W.

22
4
IN CELESTIAL NAVIGATION YOUR LANDMARKS ARE IN THE SKY!

DO not be awed by the words "celestial navigation." It is not as difficult as it sounds. In fact, you use the same principles and most of the same methods you have been using before. You take bearings on the sun, the moon, the planets, and stars in the same manner that you have been taking bearings on the poplar tree, the sea buoy, and the water tower.

The only basic difference is that in coastwise navigation the objects you sighted were stationary and were set upon the chart in their exact positions. In celestial navigation the objects you sight are in constant motion, and you must determine where they are at the time you sight, or *shoot*, them.

In coastwise navigation you found the position of the sighted object on the chart. In celestial navigation you find the position of the heavenly bodies in an *almanac*. You take this information to a set of tables, do a little addition or subtraction, and then plot a line of position exactly as you did when you took a sight on that lighthouse.

This line of position is exactly the same as the lines of position you have been studying. It can be crossed with any other line of position for a fix.

Let us return to the poplar tree on page 1.

As you walk toward the tree, the top of it appears to go higher. As you back away from it, it appears to get lower. As it goes higher you must lift your eyes to follow it; as it goes lower you must lower your eyes to keep it in sight.

We are now, in fact, dealing with a vertical angle instead of a horizontal angle. And we now use a different kind of instrument to measure the angle. This instrument is the *sextant*. It does the same thing a protractor does except that it measures the angle from the body in the sky to the ground or the horizon.

In your imagination, take the sextant and measure the angle from the top of the tree to the ground when you are standing 100 feet from the tree trunk. Let us say this proves to be 40°.

As you walked toward the tree the angle grew greater; as you walked away the angle grew smaller. But whenever you were 100 feet from the tree the angle was 40°.

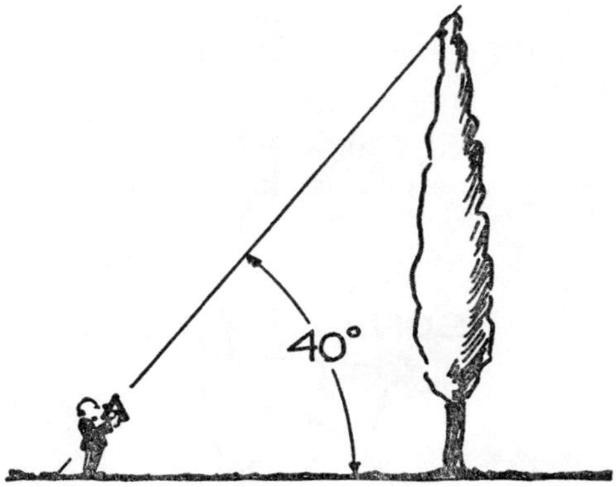

Now walk aimlessly around the tree.

Whenever you are less than 100 feet away the angle is more than 40°; whenever you are further than 100 feet away the angle is smaller than 40°.

But no matter where you are in the area, whenever the angle is 40° you are exactly 100 feet from the tree.

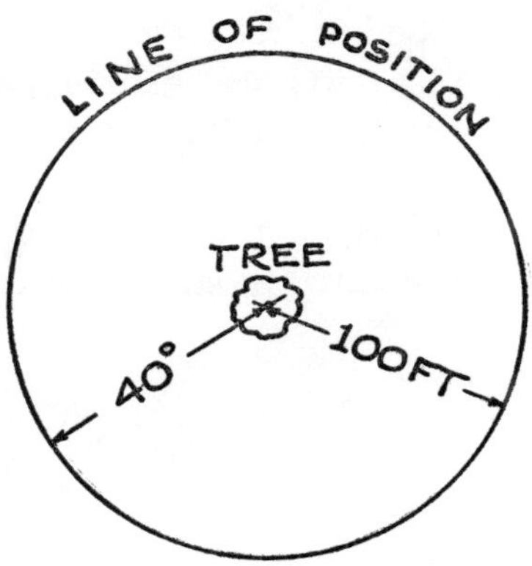

Therefore, whenever the sextant angle is 40° you are on a line of position that is 100 feet in radius around the tree. Of course the line of position is circular and not straight like our coastwise lines of position, but nevertheless it is a true line of position.

When you shoot the sun in celestial navigation, you are measuring its angle with the horizon.

Say, again, that this angle proves to be 40°.

You are obviously on a circular line of position around the sun of 40°.

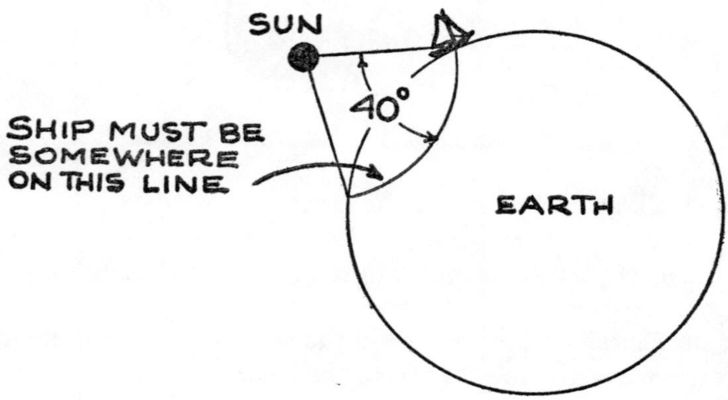

This circular line will be hundreds, maybe thousands of miles in diameter. In fact, the circle is so great that it appears on the chart as a straight line. But still it is the same kind of line of position that encircles the poplar tree.

In the center of the circle the sun stands directly above, just as the top of the poplar tree was directly above the center of the circle about its base.

If we know where the sun is we can tell where the line of position is. Now the problem is to place the sun.

If we could, like Joshua, command the sun to stand still our problem would be easy. Unfortunately the sun is never still, but is streaking across the sky at a speed of 900 knots and slowly weaving back and forth across the equator.

So now let us see how the navigator goes about fixing the position of the sun and other celestial bodies, and how he uses that information to plot his line of position.

TIME is the heart of celestial navigation, for only by knowing the exact time—even to seconds—can we determine the position of the sun and stars.

For that purpose the navigator carries with him an accurate timepiece. Frequent radio time signals have done away with the need of a delicate and expensive chronometer, except on long voyages far away from land. The most frequent source of time is the hourly "beep" on most radio programs—which is accurate to a fifth of a second—although large ships crossing the ocean procure their time checks from short-wave time signals. These are broadcast over several stations by the naval observatory.

Just as all longitude begins at Greenwich, so does all navigation time. Every navigation timepiece in the world is set to the time at Greenwich. This is known as *Greenwich Civil Time* (*GCT*), and is based on the average time the sun crosses the Greenwich meridian each day.

Eastern Standard Time (*EST*) is 5 hours later than Greenwich time, for it is based on the average daily time the sun crosses the center of its time zone. *Central Standard Time* (*CST*) is 6 hours later for the same reason. *Mountain Standard Time* (*MST*) is 7 hours later and *Pacific Standard Time* (*PST*) 8 hours later.

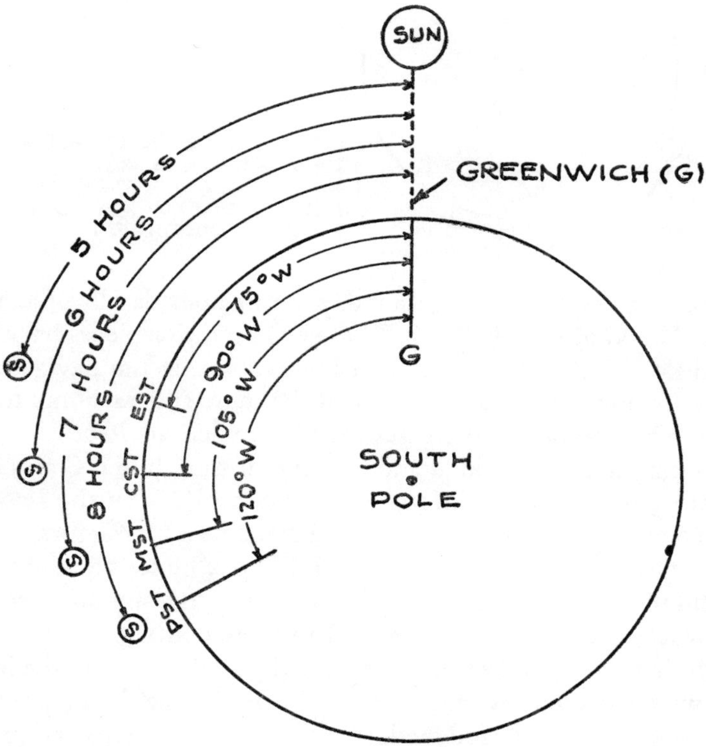

Every hour of the day and night the sun moves 15° and crosses the central meridian of another time zone. When it crosses the 180° meridian, which is in the middle of the Pacific Ocean, it is midnight in Greenwich and another navigation day begins. This is important to remember because the almanac is dated on the Greenwich day and timed by Greenwich time.

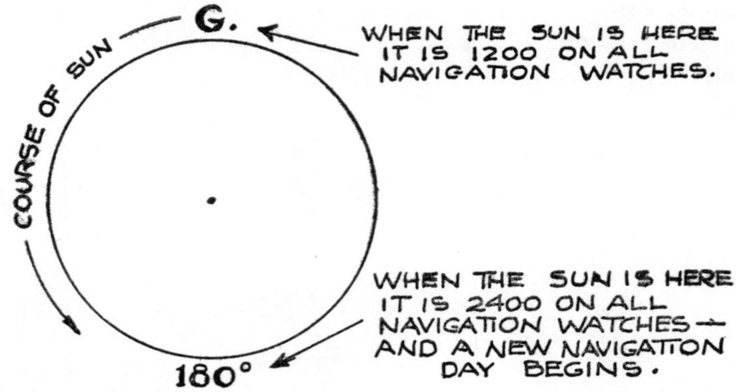

For convenience the navigation day is a 24-hour day like the military day of World War II. Modern navigation timepieces have 24-hour dials and the almanac has 24-hour tables. If the navigator is using a timepiece with a 12-hour dial, he must add 12 hours to his time shown when the sun crosses the Greenwich meridian.

In setting a watch from standard time in the United States, the navigator adds the time difference to obtain GCT. In the Eastern Time zone he adds 5 hours, in the CST zone he adds 6 hours, in the MST zone he adds 7 hours, and in the PST zone he adds 8 hours.

Naturally he must also consider whether the sun has crossed Greenwich, and if it has, he must add 12 more hours.

Right here is as good a time as any for the reader to form the habit of drawing a diagram whenever he works with time. It is a practice that should never be abandoned, for it not only prevents errors but allows the navigator to *see* the problem.

A time diagram starts with a circle representing the earth as seen from the South Pole. This angle is taken so that we will be looking toward north and west will be on our left and east on our right, or in the positions they are on maps and charts.

At the top we draw in Greenwich (or G), and to the center we draw the Greenwich meridian. Directly below we mark the 180° location. Like this:

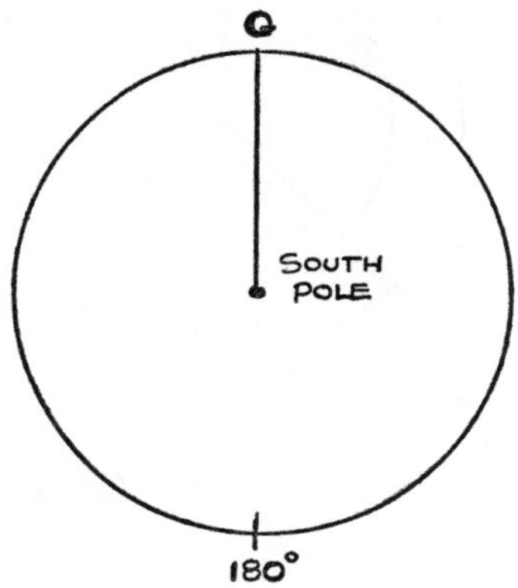

Let us say the time is 1600 GCT. That would mean the sun is four hours or 60° west of Greenwich. We draw the sun and the 60° meridian like this:

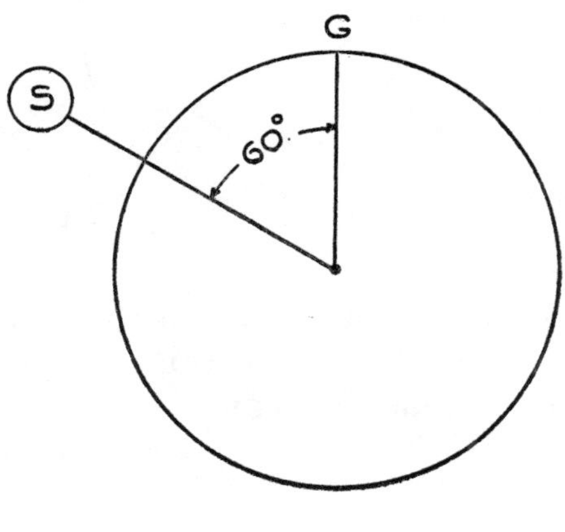

This angle is known as the *Greenwich Hour Angle* (*GHA*) and its determination is the first step in working out a celestial sight.

Let us look at some more Greenwich Hour Angles. Here is the GHA when the GCT is 2100.

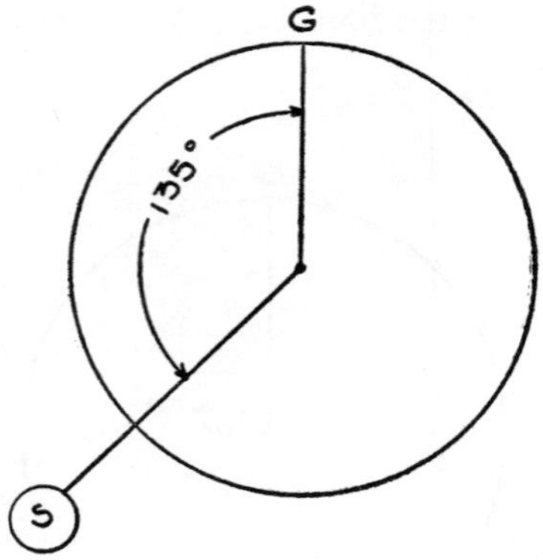

And now (watch this one) when the GCT is 0200.

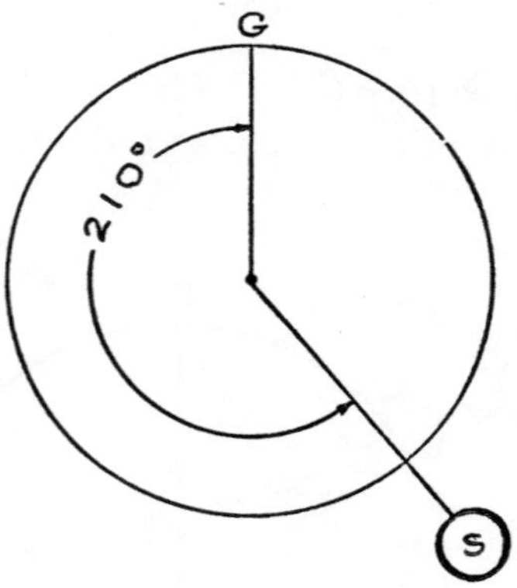

The GHA does not stop when the sun crosses the 180° meridian and another navigation day begins. It continues on until the sun crosses the Greenwich meridian again.

Here are three more examples:

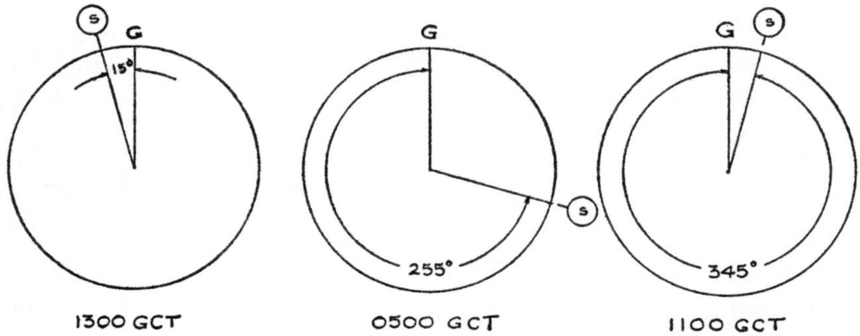

You can see that GHA is nothing more than west longitude carried on around the world. If you live at 76 34W and the sun's GHA is 76°34′, then it is on your meridian. If you live in east longitude you can always find the GHA of your meridian by subtracting it from 360°. For instance, if your meridian is 24 16E its GHA is 360° less 24°16′, or 335°44′.

It would have been far simpler for everyone had GHA been adopted for measuring the earth instead of east and west longitude, but the geographers had laid out the world by longitude long before the navigators came along.

The chief job of the almanac is to tell you the GHA of the sun, moon, planets, and stars for every hour, minute, and second of the day.

AFTER the navigator has found the GHA from the almanac, has jotted down the figures, and has drawn it in the time diagram, he figures out the *Local Hour Angle* (*LHA*), which is the distance the sun or star is from *his* meridian.

Let us go back to the time diagram and, for example, say that the GHA of the sun is 47°.

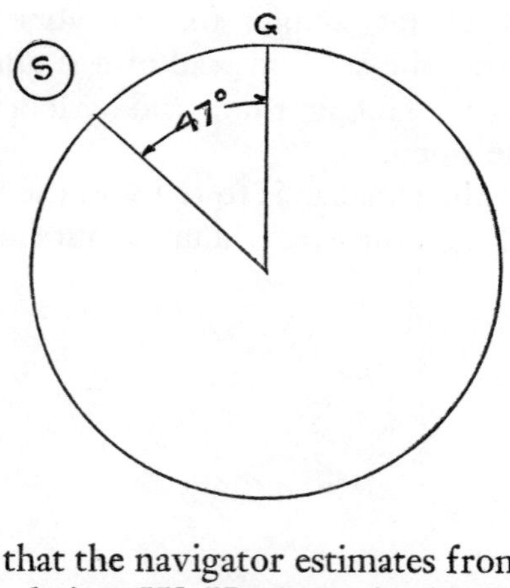

Now let us say that the navigator estimates from his dead reckoning that his longitude is 88W. He draws in this meridian (M stands for the local meridian). The time diagram then will look like this:

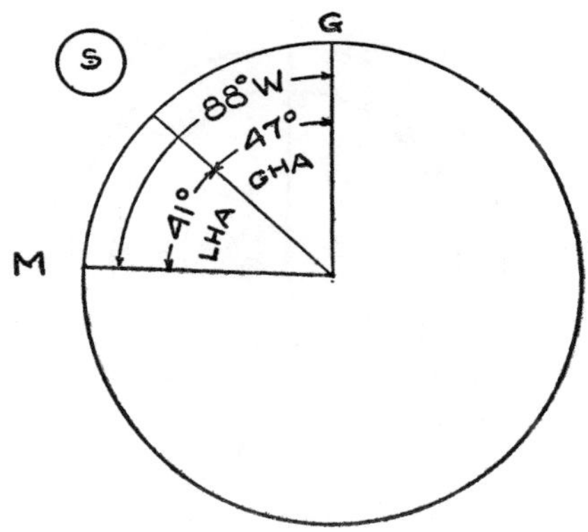

Simple arithmetic will show you that the LHA in this case must be the difference between 88° and 47°, or 41°. In other words, the navigator must be approximately 41° west of the sun's meridian.

Here is another example. Let us say the sun's GHA is 124° and the local meridian is assumed to be 82°.

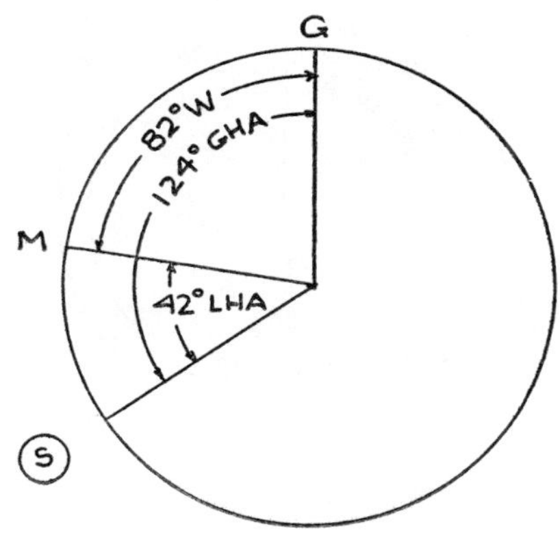

It is apparent that here we subtract the 82° from the 124° to find the LHA of 42°.

East longitude sometimes presents a slight difficulty, for we have angles running in different directions.

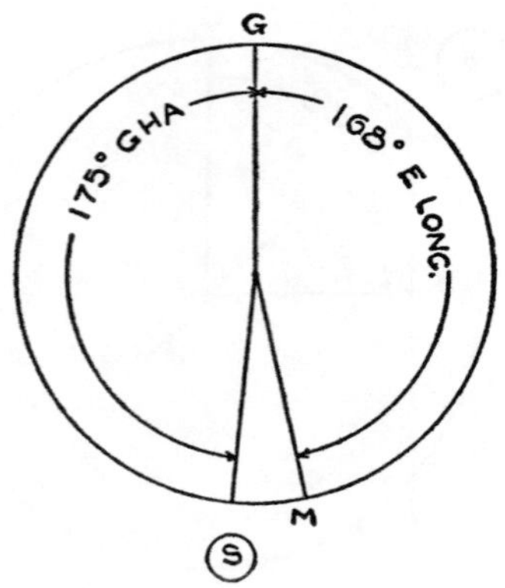

The easiest way out is to change east longitude to west longitude (or GHA) by subtracting it from 360°. In the above case, where the sun's GHA is 175° and the navigator's meridian estimated to be 168E, this is what happens:

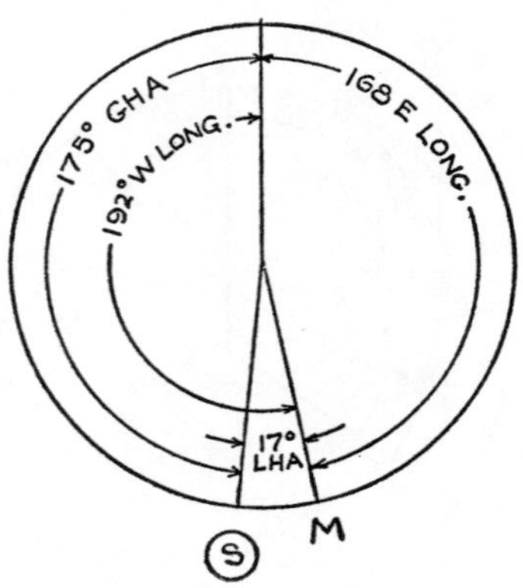

The local meridian, being east, is subtracted from 360° to give west longitude or its GHA as 192°, and simple subtraction will give the LHA of 17°.

When the sun is west of Greenwich and the navigator is in east longitude, the diagram shows you that the angles must be added, like this:

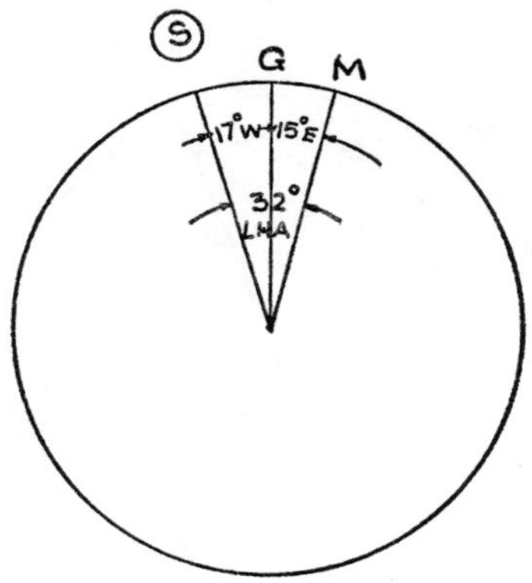

When the sun is east of Greenwich and the navigator is west the result may look like this:

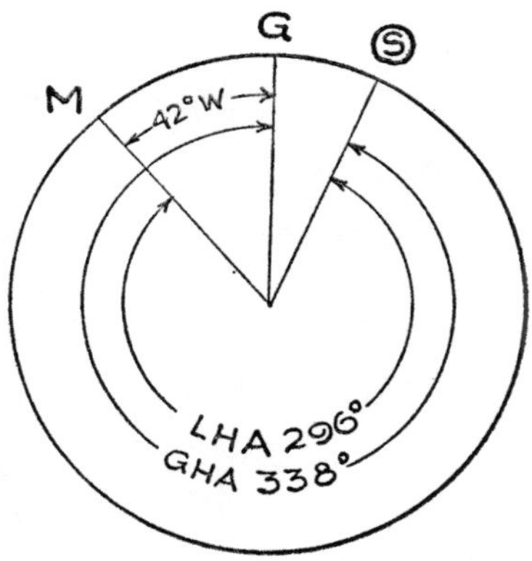

The LHA is 338° minus 42°, or 296°. But this is an unhandy figure for we are measuring an angle three-fourths around the world. Besides that we are interested in getting the shorter angle because navigation tables only carry angles of less than 180°.

We simply subtract the LHA of 296° from our old friend 360° for—

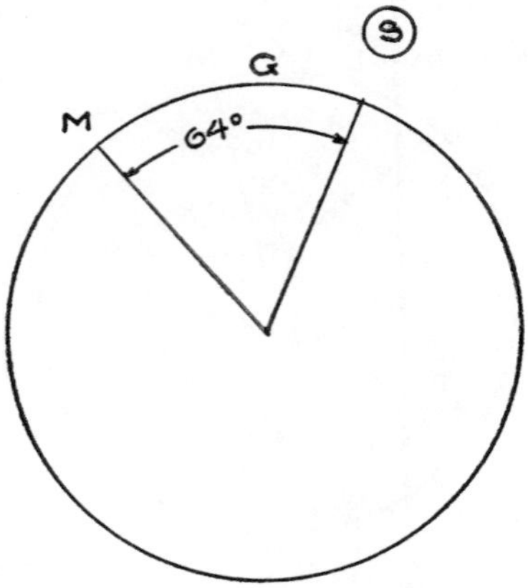

—the smaller angle of 64°.

As you can see there are many rules—if we were rule-minded—we could give you for finding LHA. But the simplest and safest way is to draw the time diagram every time you work a sight so that you can *see* what's happening.

Then plain horse sense will show you what to do.

Here are a few random diagrams:

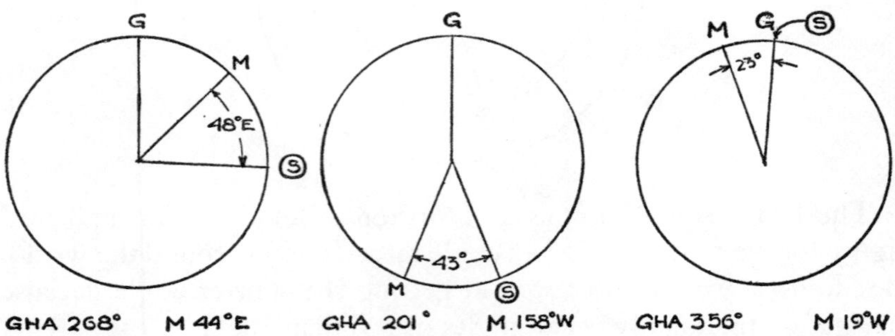

YOU have seen how location on the earth is found or established by lines of latitude and longitude, and how every spot on the globe is so many degrees north or south of the equator and so many degrees east or west of Greenwich.

And you have seen how the sun and other heavenly bodies are located in their east to west movement by their Greenwich Hour Angle (GHA), which is their distance west of Greenwich. That, in so many words, is their longitude.

Now these bodies, like locations on the earth, have also their latitude, or distance north or south of the equator—except for reasons best known to astronomers, instead of it being called latitude, it is called *declination.*

As far as we are concerned, latitude and declination are the same thing.

When the almanac says the sun's declination at a certain time is 14° 16N, that means that the sun is that far north of the equator. If you were standing at any spot that was 14 16N, the sun that day would pass directly over your head.

Let us say you were at 14 16N and 78 24W. The sun would be overhead when its GHA was 78°24'.

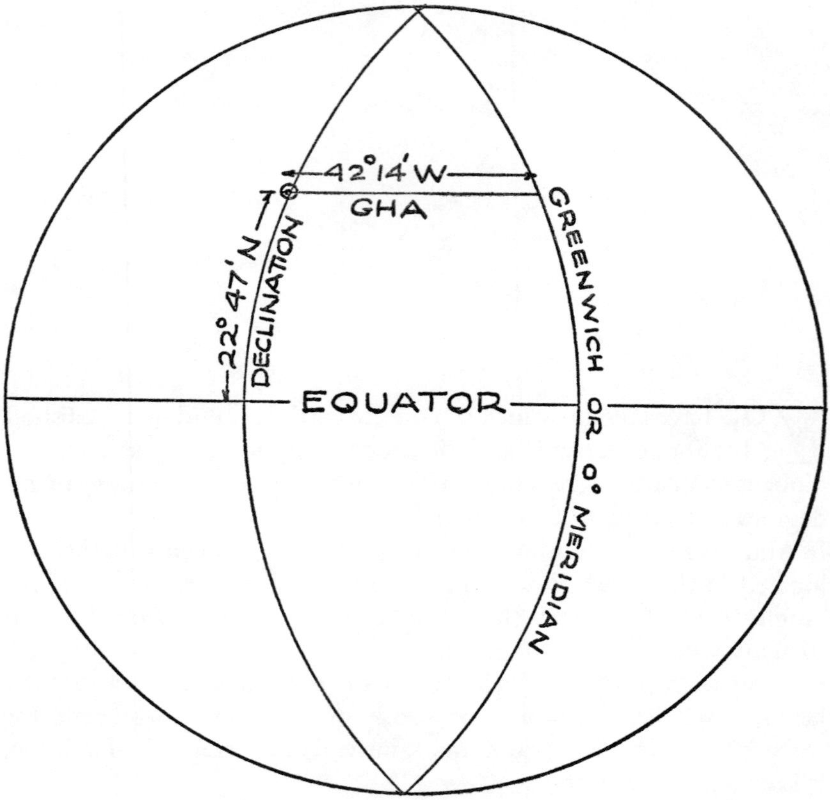

GHA = LONGITUDE
DECLINATION = LATITUDE

On the page to your left is another example graphically described. The location is 22 47N, 42 14W. See that the lines of GHA and declination are exactly the same as the lines of longitude and latitude.

The sun never goes any further north or south than 23°27′, so actually it can never be directly overhead in any part of continental United States. The same is true of the planets, although the moon may come as far north as 28°30′, the southern tip of Florida or Texas.

The stars have no limit to their declination and some, like Polaris or the Pole Star, live constantly above the polar region.

The speed of change in declination of the heavenly bodies is very slight as compared to their change in GHA. The moon may change 15′ or 16′ in an hour, the sun and planets 1′ every two or three hours, but the change in the stars is so slow that some of them keep the same declination for years.

Here is a step in practical celestial navigation—when a star is directly overhead (which is called your *zenith*) its declination will tell you your latitude and its GHA will tell you your longitude. There's your fix!

(But, alas, it is impossible to determine zenith from the deck of a rocking boat or the cockpit of a lunging airplane. So you had better keep on reading the next few pages.)

BUT at this point you might well ask, "If we know the geographical position of the sun, and our sextant will tell us our angular distance from it, why can't we just measure the distance and draw our line of position at that point?"

Well, we could if the distances weren't so considerable. But we can't get navigational accuracy on a chart that is several thousand miles wide. Another thing, the earth is curved and only a small portion can safely be transferred to a flat chart. So we must resort to a trick or two.

Let us go back to the poplar tree.

Remember, we knew that at a distance of 100 feet from the base the sextant angle for the top was 40°. Now let us say that we also knew that every change of one minute of angle meant a difference of 2 feet over the ground.

On one occasion we shot the top of the tree and the sextant reading was 40° 08′.

Here is what we reason:

1. The angle is larger than 40°, therefore we must be *toward* the tree from the 100-foot line of position.

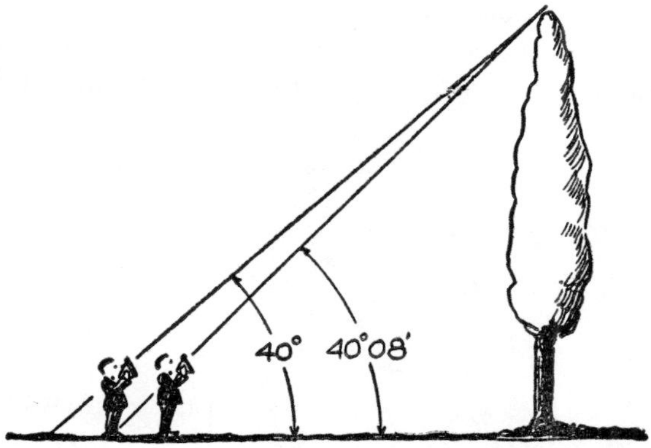

2. Our sextant reading was 8′ more than 40°.
3. Every change of 1′ means a change over the ground of 2 feet.
4. Therefore, we must be on a line of position that is 16 feet *toward* the tree.

Now in navigation we do not have these poplar tree measurements in such handy form as in this example, but we do have similar distance measurements in the navigation tables, worked out for us by countless mathematicians, so that we can work sights with little effort.

After we have taken a sight on the sun and looked up its position in the almanac, we say to the tables:

"I don't know where I am exactly, but I will *assume* that I am at so many degrees latitude and so many degrees longitude. If I were at that spot and the sun's LHA was so and so and its declination so and so, what should my sextant read?"

The tables come back at us with this:

"With what you have told me your sextant reading should be so and so and the bearing (or *azimuth*) of the sun from you is so many degrees."

Now if our sextant reading is the same as the one told us by the tables, then the ship must be on the same line of position as would cut through the *assumed* position.

In that case we would draw a line of position through the assumed position at *right angles* to the bearing or azimuth of the sun and we would be on that line.

But the tables very rarely give the same reading that we have taken of the sun. Let us say our reading was 50°16′ and the tables' answer for the assumed position was 50°28′.

Then we know we are on a line of position 12′ or 12 miles from the assumed line of position, and as our reading is smaller than that of the tables, we must be on a line of position 12 miles *away* from the assumed line of position.

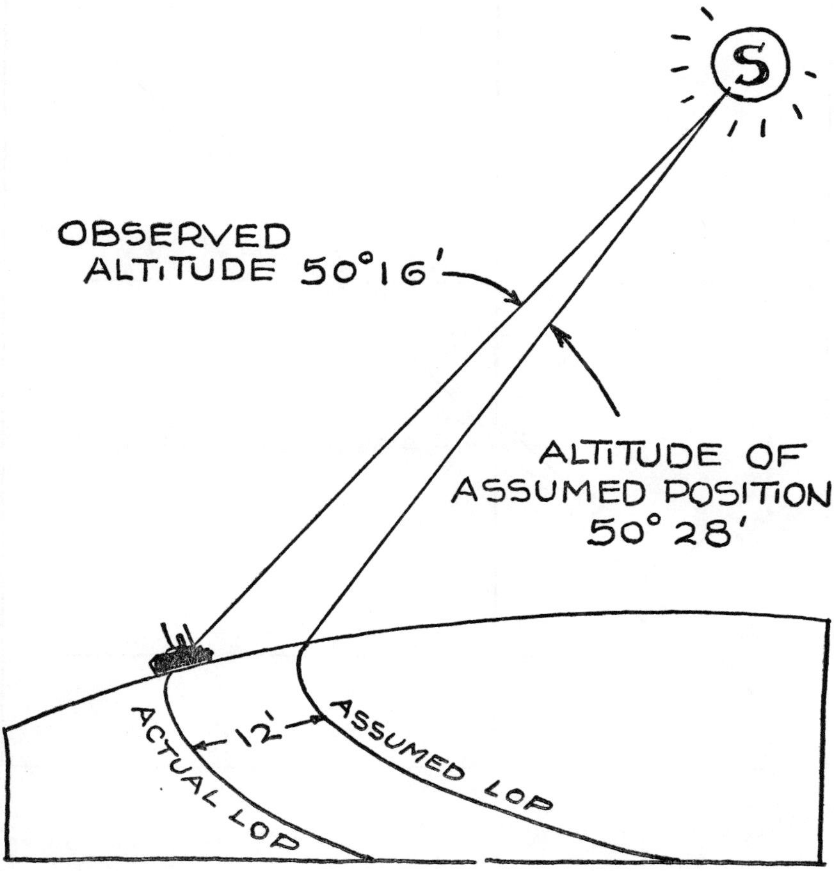

Now we are ready to plot the line of position. We draw the azimuth line as given in the tables the same way we drew the lighthouse bearing in the early part of this book, except that we draw it from the assumed position toward the sun.

But we are *away*, or on the other side of this line, so we continue it through the assumed position for a distance of 12 miles. At exactly 12 miles from the assumed position on the azimuth line we draw a line of position at right angles to it.

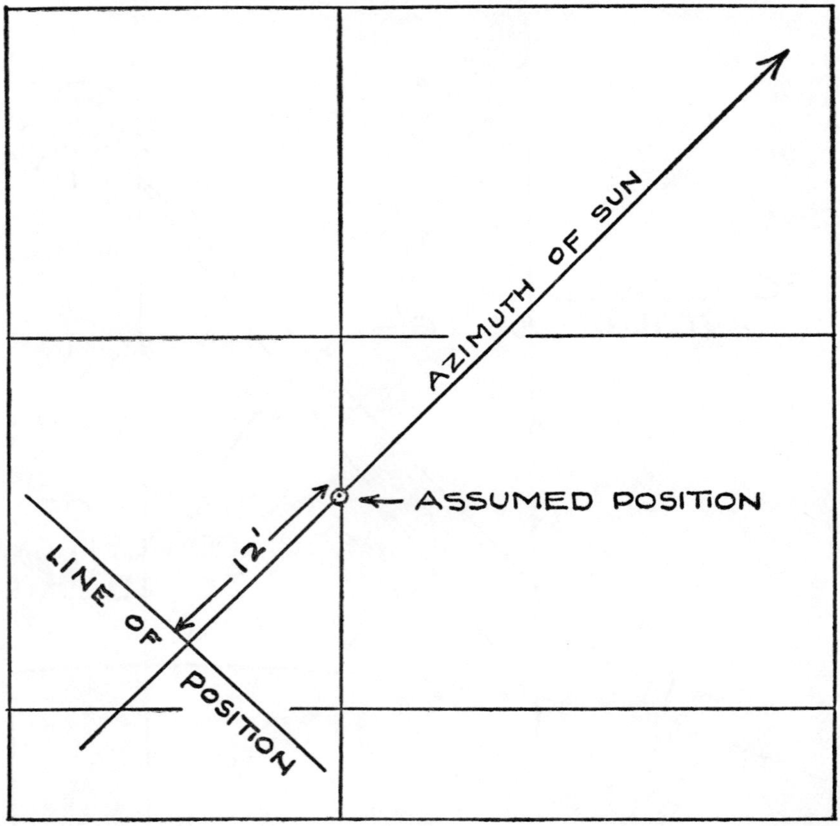

We are somewhere on that line.

THE pages you have just read described the principles of modern celestial navigation (which incidentally bears the high-sounding title of Determination of the Sumner Line of Position by the Marq St.-Hilaire Method). Now we will take up the mechanics of the process step by step.

Say we have decided to take a sun sight. As the exact second must be noted at the time we shoot the sun, we station someone next to the chronometer or timepiece, or have him set his watch to it and hold it near-by us. If we are alone we set a stop watch at a certain minute and punch the stop mechanism at the instant of the sight, adding the elapsed time to the time we started it.

To be on the safe side we take several shots, noting the exact time on each, until we feel that we have a good one. (Don't ask us how to tell that—it's a sixth sense and you will feel it when you start practicing sights.)

If you have someone keeping time for you it's customary to let him do all the bookkeeping. When you have taken your sight you call out "Time," then read your sight and give it to him. He jots down the time, then opposite it puts down the sextant reading.

As we said before, a sextant is nothing more than an instrument for reading angles. Basically it is the same as a protractor. In fact, a protractor can be used as a sort of emergency sextant and was done so many times by lifeboat survivors in World War II.

The sextant, by a simple system of mirrors, gives us the angle of a celestial body from the horizon.

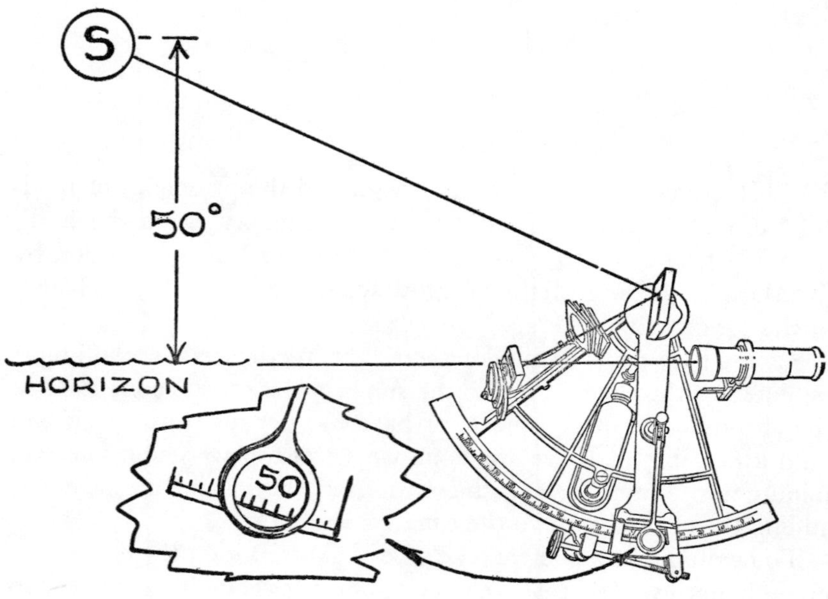

The degrees and minutes of the angle are read from a vernier scale on the bottom of the sextant, or in the newest type instruments, on a micrometer screw drum.

When we look through the sighting tube of the sextant we see a glass square, one half of which is a mirror and reflects the view of the top mirror, and the other half transparent. In shooting a celestial object we point the sextant so that we see the horizon in the transparent glass, then move the arm, to which the top mirror is attached, until the object is level with the horizon.

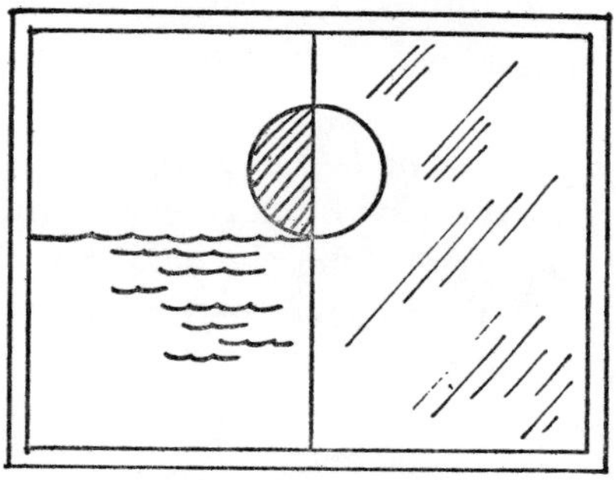

In the case of the sun or moon, we "bring down" the disc until the bottom or *lower limb* is in line with the horizon. Naturally, a star or planet has no visible diameter.

The indicator of the arm against the scale, or the drum of the micrometer, gives us the altitude of the object. This reading is called the *sextant altitude* (*Hs*).

This reading, however, is worthless until certain errors are corrected.

First is the probable error of the sextant itself, caused by numerous physical conditions, such as temperature, wear, maladjustment, etc.

This is known as the *Index Error* (*I.E.*) and is found by the navigator before he takes a sight. The sextant is sighted on the horizon and the arm moved until the mirror is also on the horizon. The two images are lined up and the scale read. If the instrument has no error the reading will be zero. Whatever it reads other than that is applied in the *opposite* way to the reading. For instance, if the scale reads 2′ above zero, then the sextant has an error of plus 2′, and to correct any reading 2′ must be subtracted from it. If the error is below zero then the correction is added. This is known as the *Index Correction* (*I.C.*).

The next correction is for *Dip* or *Height of Eye*. This is because the horizon drops or dips as your eye gets higher. This error is always figured on your height plus the height of the deck of the ship above the waterline. To correct for dip the error is always subtracted from the reading.

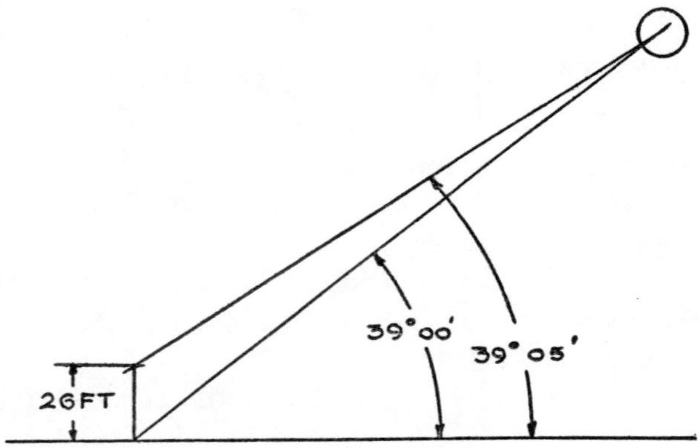

Refraction is another error that must always be corrected. It is caused by the bending of the light rays from celestial bodies by the earth's atmosphere, and it increases as the altitude of the body is lower. Do you remember how a stick half way in the water seems to bend below the surface of the water? That's what happens to light rays when they encounter our atmosphere. This correction is always subtracted.

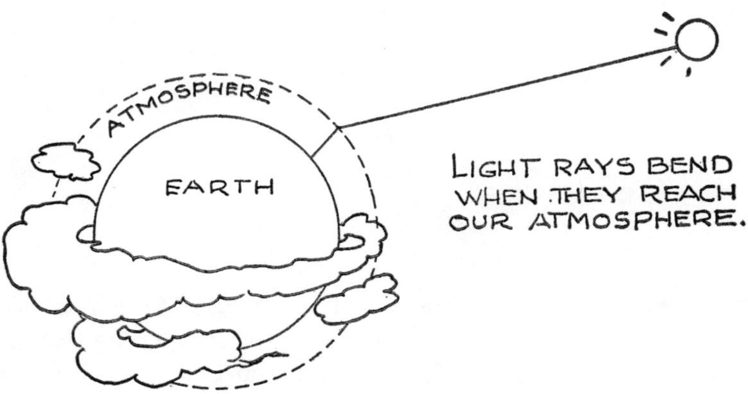

ATMOSPHERE
EARTH
LIGHT RAYS BEND
WHEN THEY REACH
OUR ATMOSPHERE.

These three corrections are basic and must be applied to *all* sextant readings. In the case of sights of the stars and planets, that is all the correction necessary. However, with the sun and moon, because of their relative nearness and their apparent size, we must apply two more corrections to a moon sight and one more to a sun sight.

The first is *semi-diameter*. This error exists because we generally sight the bottom (*lower limb*) or top (*upper limb*) of the sun and moon rather than the center, and we must add or subtract the distance from the edge of the sun or moon to the center. If we line up the lower limb, which we do 99 out of 100 times, we *add* the semi-diameter; if we line up the upper limb, which is sometimes done because a cloud is obscuring part of the object, we *subtract* it.

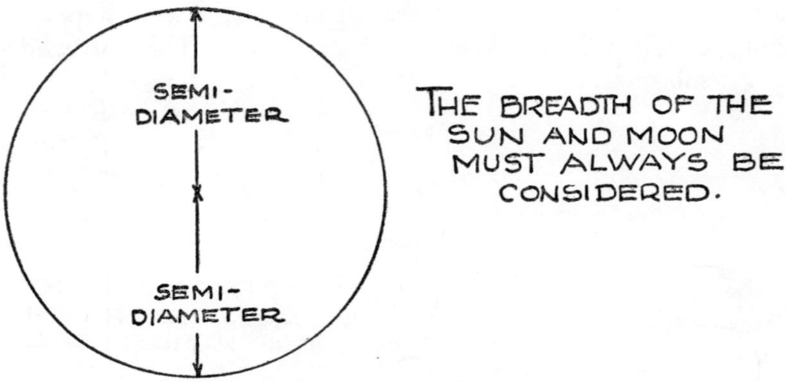
SEMI-
DIAMETER
SEMI-
DIAMETER
THE BREADTH OF THE SUN AND MOON MUST ALWAYS BE CONSIDERED.

The last error, *parallax*, is used only in the case of the moon sight; in the case of the sun this error amounts to about a tenth of a minute and is generally disregarded. But the moon being a mere stone's throw, astronomically speaking, it presents a unique problem.

Naturally, the authors of the navigation tables do not know where you are. So for the sake of argument they say you are in the center of the earth. This makes no difference in the case of the stars and planets because they are so far away that the distance between the surface of the earth, where you actually are, and the center of the earth, where the mathematicians say you are, is so slight, in comparison, that it is microscopic.

But it matters very much in the case of the moon, causing an error as high as 61′, or over a degree. Parallax is always *added* to the reading.

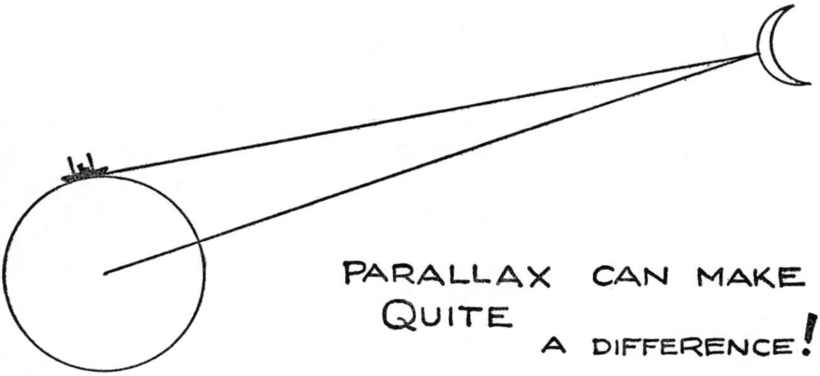
PARALLAX CAN MAKE
QUITE
A DIFFERENCE!

Now here is where you will find the corrections:

Index Correction (I.C.). This you find yourself by sighting the horizon and lining it up both in the transparent glass and in the mirror. If the scale does not read zero, what it does read must be applied to later readings—in *reverse.*

Dip or Height of Eye. On the back cover of the Air Almanac. On the last pages of the Nautical Almanac. On the inside cover of any government navigation table. This correction is *subtracted.*

Refraction. Same as above. This correction is *subtracted.*

Semi-Diameter. That of the sun is always 16′. The moon's semi-diameter is given in the last column on each daily page of the Air Almanac. This correction is always *added* when the lower limb is sighted; *subtracted* when the upper limb is sighted.

Parallax. The moon's parallax is found on the last column of each daily page of the Air Almanac. This correction is always *added.*

When all corrections have been applied to the sextant reading (*Hs*), it is known as the *observed altitude* (*Ho*).

LET us go back now to that sun sight we were taking. Say we are on a ship in the mid-Atlantic. It is about eight o'clock in the morning, ship's time, on March 4, 1949. By dead reckoning we estimate our position to be 31 14N, 51 32W. We figure our height of eye to be 26 feet and have found that the index correction should be —2′.

At GCT 11h 14m 12s we shoot the lower limb of the sun for an Hs of 16° 46′.

First we correct the sextant reading, using the correction tables in the Air Almanac.

Hs	16°46′
I.C.	— 2′
Dip	— 5′
Refraction	— 4′
Semi-Diameter	+16′
Ho	16°51′

Momentarily we put this aside and pick up the Air Almanac. This book is published for every four months of the year, two pages (one

GCT	☉ SUN GHA	☉ SUN Dec.	♈ GHA	VENUS −3.4 GHA	VENUS −3.4 Dec.	JUPITER −1.5 GHA	JUPITER −1.5 Dec.	SATURN 0.4 GHA	SATURN 0.4 Dec.	MOON GHA	MOON Dec.
h m	° ′	° ′	° ′	° ′	° ′	° ′	° ′	° ′	° ′	° ′	° ′
0 00	177 00	S 6 39	161 25	186 58	S11 58	225 38	S21 27	6 48	N12 27	135 42	N10 48
10	179 30		163 56	189 28		228 08		9 18		138 08	50
20	182 00		166 26	191 58		230 38		11 48		140 34	53
30	184 30	• •	168 57	194 28	• •	233 09	• •	14 19	• •	143 00	• 55
40	187 00		171 27	196 58		235 39		16 49		145 26	57
50	189 30		173 57	199 27		238 09		19 20		147 52	10 59
1 00	192 00	S 6 38	176 28	201 57	S11 57	240 40	S21 27	21 50	N12 27	150 18	N11 01
10	194 30		178 58	204 27		243 10		24 21		152 43	03
20	197 00		181 29	206 57		245 40		26 51		155 09	06
30	199 30	• •	183 59	209 27	• •	248 11	• •	29 22	• •	157 35	• 08
40	202 00		186 29	211 57		250 41		31 52		160 01	10
50	204 30		189 00	214 27		253 11		34 22		162 27	12
2 00	207 00	S 6 37	191 30	216 57	S11 56	255 42	S21 27	36 53	N12 27	164 53	N11 14
10	209 30		194 01	219 27		258 12		39 23		167 19	17
20	212 00		196 31	221 57		260 42		41 54		169 45	19
30	214 30	• •	199 02	224 27	• •	263 13	• •	44 24	• •	172 10	• 21
40	217 00		201 32	226 56		265 43		46 55		174 36	23
50	219 30		204 02	229 26		268 13		49 25		177 02	25
3 00	222 01	S 6 36	206 33	231 56	S11 55	270 43	S21 27	51 56	N12 27	179 28	N11 27
10	224 31		209 03	234 26		273 14		54 26		181 54	30
20	227 01		211 34	236 56		275 44		56 56		184 20	32
30	229 31	• •	214 04	239 26	• •	278 14	• •	59 27	• •	186 45	• 34
40	232 01		216 34	241 56		280 45		61 57		189 11	36
50	234 31		219 05	244 26		283 15		64 28		191 37	38
4 00	237 01	S 6 35	221 35	246 56	S11 54	285 45	S21 27	66 58	N12 27	194 03	N11 41
10	239 31		224 06	249 26		288 16		69 29		196 29	43
20	242 01		226 36	251 56		290 46		71 59		198 55	45
30	244 31	• •	229 06	254 25	• •	293 16	• •	74 30	• •	201 21	• 47
40	247 01		231 37	256 55		295 47		77 00		203 46	49
50	249 31		234 07	259 25		298 17		79 30		206 12	51
5 00	252 01	S 6 34	236 38	261 55	S11 53	300 47	S21 27	82 01	N12 27	208 38	N11 53
10	254 31		239 08	264 25		303 18		84 31		211 04	56
20	257 01		241 38	266 55		305 48		87 02		213 30	11 58
30	259 31	• •	244 09	269 25	• •	308 18	• •	89 32	• •	215 56	12 00
40	262 01		246 39	271 55		310 49		92 03		218 21	02
50	264 31		249 10	274 25		313 19		94 33		220 47	04
6 00	267 01	S 6 33	251 40	276 55	S11 52	315 49	S21 26	97 04	N12 27	223 13	N12 06
10	269 31		254 11	279 25		318 20		99 34		225 39	09
20	272 01		256 41	281 55		320 50		102 04		228 05	11
30	274 31	• •	259 11	284 24	• •	323 20	• •	104 35	• •	230 30	• 13
40	277 01		261 42	286 54		325 51		107 05		232 56	15
50	279 31		264 12	289 24		328 21		109 36		235 22	• 17
7 00	282 01	S 6 32	266 43	291 54	S11 51	330 51	S21 26	112 06	N12 27	237 48	N12 19
10	284 31		269 13	294 24		333 22		114 37		240 14	21
20	287 01		271 43	296 54		335 52		117 07		242 40	24
30	289 31	• •	274 14	299 24	• •	338 22	• •	119 37	• •	245 05	• 26
40	292 01		276 44	301 54		340 53		122 08		247 31	28
50	294 31		279 15	304 24		343 23		124 38		249 57	30
8 00	297 01	S 6 31	281 45	306 54	S11 49	345 53	S21 26	127 09	N12 27	252 23	N12 32
10	299 31		284 15	309 24		348 24		129 39		254 49	34
20	302 01		286 46	311 53		350 54		132 10		257 14	36
30	304 31	• •	289 16	314 23	• •	353 24	• •	134 40	• •	259 40	• 39
40	307 01		291 47	316 53		355 55		137 11		262 06	41
50	309 31		294 17	319 23		358 25		139 41		264 32	43
9 00	312 01	S 6 30	296 48	321 53	S11 48	0 55	S21 26	142 11	N12 27	266 58	N12 45
10	314 31		299 18	324 23		3 26		144 42		269 23	47
20	317 01		301 48	326 53		5 56		147 12		271 49	49
30	319 31	• •	304 19	329 23	• •	8 26	• •	149 43	• •	274 15	• 51
40	322 01		306 49	331 53		10 57		152 13		276 41	53
50	324 31		309 20	334 23		13 27		154 44		279 07	56
10 00	327 02	S 6 29	311 50	336 53	S11 47	15 57	S21 26	157 14	N12 27	281 32	N12 58
10	329 32		314 20	339 23		18 28		159 45		283 58	13 00
20	332 02		316 51	341 52		20 58		162 15		286 24	02
30	334 32	• •	319 21	344 22	• •	23 28	• •	164 45	• •	288 50	• 04
40	337 02		321 52	346 52		25 59		167 16		291 15	06
50	339 32		324 22	349 22		28 29		169 46		293 41	08
11 00	342 02	S 6 28	326 52	351 52	S11 46	30 59	S21 26	172 17	N12 27	296 07	N13 10
10	344 32		329 23	354 22		33 30		174 47		298 33	13
20	347 02		331 53	356 52		36 00		177 18		300 59	15
30	349 32	• •	334 24	359 22	• •	38 30	• •	179 48	• •	303 24	• 17
40	352 02		336 54	1 52		41 01		182 19		305 50	19
50	354 32		339 25	4 22		43 31		184 49		308 16	21
12 00	357 02	S 6 27	341 55	6 52	S11 45	46 01	S21 26	187 19	N12 27	310 42	N13 23

☾ Par.

° Alt.	′ + Corr.
0	
	54
10	
	53
15	
	52
18	
	51
21	
	50
24	
	49
26	
	48
29	
	47
31	
	46
33	
	45
35	
	44
36	
	43
38	
	42
40	
	41
41	
	40
43	
	39
44	
	38
46	
	37
47	
	36
49	
	35
50	
	34
51	
	33
53	
	32
54	
	31
55	
	30
57	
	29
58	
	28
59	
	27
60	
	26
62	
	25
63	
	24
64	
	23
65	
	22
66	
	21
67	
	20
68	
	19
70	
	18
71	
	17
72	
	16
73	
	15
74	
	14
75	
	13
76	
	12
77	
	11
78	
	10
79	

SD ☉ ′ 16

SD ☾ ′ 15

Corr. HA ☾

m Int.	′ Corr.
0	
	0
5	
	+1
10	

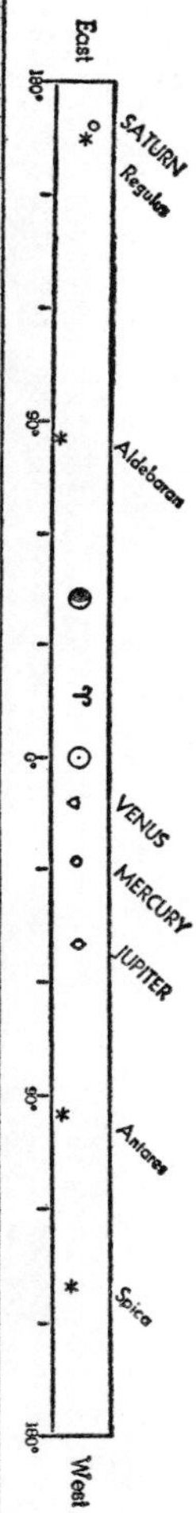

GCT	☉ SUN GHA	SUN Dec.	♈ GHA	VENUS −3.4 GHA	VENUS Dec.	JUPITER −1.5 GHA	JUPITER Dec.	SATURN 0.4 GHA	SATURN Dec.	◐ MOON GHA	MOON Dec.
h m	° ′	° ′	° ′	° ′	° ′	° ′	° ′	° ′	° ′	° ′	° ′
12 00	357 02	S 6 27	341 55	6 52	S11 45	46 01	S21 26	187 19	N12 27	310 42	N13 23
10	359 32		344 25	9 21		48 32		189 50		313 07	25
20	2 02		346 56	11 51		51 02		192 20		315 33	27
30	4 32	• •	349 26	14 21	• •	53 32	• •	194 51	• •	317 59	• 29
40	7 02		351 57	16 51		56 02		197 21		320 25	32
50	9 32		354 27	19 21		58 33		199 52		322 50	34
13 00	12 02	S 6 26	356 57	21 51	S11 44	61 03	S21 26	202 22	N12 28	325 16	N13 36
10	14 32		359 28	24 21		63 33		204 53		327 42	38
20	17 02		1 58	26 51		66 04		207 23		330 08	40
30	19 32	• •	4 29	29 21	• •	68 34	• •	209 53	• •	332 33	• 42
40	22 02		6 59	31 51		71 04		212 24		334 59	44
50	24 32		9 29	34 21		73 35		214 54		337 25	46
14 00	27 02	S 6 25	12 00	36 51	S11 43	76 05	S21 26	217 25	N12 28	339 51	N13 48
10	29 32		14 30	39 20		78 35		219 55		342 16	50
20	32 02		17 01	41 50		81 06		222 26		344 42	53
30	34 32	• •	19 31	44 20	• •	83 36	• •	224 56	• •	347 08	• 55
40	37 02		22 01	46 50		86 06		227 26		349 34	57
50	39 32		24 32	49 20		88 37		229 57		351 59	13 59
15 00	42 02	S 6 24	27 02	51 50	S11 42	91 07	S21 26	232 27	N12 28	354 25	N14 01
10	44 32		29 33	54 20		93 37		234 58		356 51	03
20	47 02		32 03	56 50		96 08		237 28		359 17	05
30	49 32	• •	34 34	59 20	• •	98 38	• •	239 59	• •	1 42	• 07
40	52 02		37 04	61 50		101 08		242 29		4 08	09
50	54 32		39 34	64 20		103 39		245 00		6 34	11
16 00	57 02	S 6 23	42 05	66 49	S11 41	106 09	S21 26	247 30	N12 28	9 00	N14 13
10	59 32		44 35	69 19		108 39		250 00		11 25	15
20	62 02		47 06	71 49		111 10		252 31		13 51	18
30	64 32	• •	49 36	74 19	• •	113 40	• •	255 01	• •	16 17	• 20
40	67 02		52 06	76 49		116 10		257 32		18 42	22
50	69 32		54 37	79 19		118 41		260 02		21 08	24
17 00	72 03	S 6 22	57 07	81 49	S11 40	121 11	S21 26	262 33	N12 28	23 34	N14 26
10	74 33		59 38	84 19		123 41		265 03		26 00	28
20	77 03		62 08	86 49		126 12		267 34		28 25	30
30	79 33	• •	64 38	89 19	• •	128 42	• •	270 04	• •	30 51	• 32
40	82 03		67 09	91 49		131 12		272 34		33 17	34
50	84 33		69 39	94 18		133 43		275 05		35 42	36
18 00	87 03	S 6 21	72 10	96 48	S11 39	136 13	S21 25	277 35	N12 28	38 08	N14 38
10	89 33		74 40	99 18		138 43		280 06		40 34	40
20	92 03		77 11	101 48		141 14		282 36		42 59	42
30	94 33	• •	79 41	104 18	• •	143 44	• •	285 07	• •	45 25	• 44
40	97 03		82 11	106 48		146 14		287 37		47 51	46
50	99 33		84 42	109 18		148 45		290 08		50 17	49
19 00	102 03	S 6 20	87 12	111 48	S11 38	151 15	S21 25	292 38	N12 28	52 42	N14 51
10	104 33		89 43	114 18		153 45		295 08		55 08	53
20	107 03		92 13	116 48		156 16		297 39		57 34	55
30	109 33	• •	94 43	119 18	• •	158 46	• •	300 09	• •	59 59	• 57
40	112 03		97 14	121 48		161 16		302 40		62 25	14 59
50	114 33		99 44	124 17		163 47		305 10		64 51	15 01
20 00	117 03	S 6 19	102 15	126 47	S11 36	166 17	S21 25	307 41	N12 28	67 16	N15 03
10	119 33		104 45	129 17		168 47		310 11		69 42	05
20	122 03		107 15	131 47		171 18		312 42		72 08	07
30	124 33	• •	109 46	134 17	• •	173 48	• •	315 12	• •	74 33	• 09
40	127 03		112 16	136 47		176 18		317 42		76 59	11
50	129 33		114 47	139 17		178 49		320 13		79 25	13
21 00	132 03	S 6 18	117 17	141 47	S11 35	181 19	S21 25	322 43	N12 28	81 50	N15 15
10	134 33		119 48	144 17		183 49		325 14		84 16	17
20	137 03		122 18	146 47		186 20		327 44		86 42	19
30	139 33	• •	124 48	149 17	• •	188 50	• •	330 15	• •	89 07	• 21
40	142 03		127 19	151 46		191 20		332 45		91 33	23
50	144 33		129 49	154 16		193 50		335 16		93 59	25
22 00	147 03	S 6 18	132 20	156 46	S11 34	196 21	S21 25	337 46	N12 28	96 24	N15 27
10	149 33		134 50	159 16		198 51		340 16		98 50	29
20	152 03		137 20	161 46		201 21		342 47		101 16	31
30	154 33	• •	139 51	164 16	• •	203 52	• •	345 17	• •	103 41	• 33
40	157 03		142 21	166 46		206 22		347 48		106 07	35
50	159 33		144 52	169 16		208 52		350 18		108 33	37
23 00	162 03	S 6 17	147 22	171 46	S11 33	211 23	S21 25	352 49	N12 28	110 58	N15 40
10	164 33		149 52	174 16		213 53		355 19		113 24	42
20	167 03		152 23	176 46		216 23		357 49		115 49	44
30	169 33	• •	154 53	179 16	• •	218 54	• •	0 20	• •	118 15	• 46
40	172 03		157 24	181 45		221 24		2 50		120 41	48
50	174 33		159 54	184 15		223 54		5 21		123 06	50
24 00	177 04	S 6 16	162 25	186 45	S11 32	226 25	S21 25	7 51	N12 28	125 32	N15 52

Lat.	Sunrise	Twlt.	Moonrise	Diff.
N				
°	h m	m	h m	m
70	7 15	61	6 43	*
68	09	56	6 59	*
66	7 03	52	7 12	*
64	6 59	48	23	*
62	55	46	33	*
60	52	43	41	00
58	48	40	48	04
56	46	39	7 54	08
54	43	37	8 00	10
52	41	35	05	13
50	39	34	10	15
45	34	31	20	20
40	30	28	28	24
35	27	26	36	27
30	23	25	42	30
20	18	23	8 54	34
10	13	21	9 04	39
0	09	21	13	43
10	6 04	21	22	47
20	5 59	23	33	51
30	53	24	44	56
35	50	25	51	59
40	46	27	9 59	62
45	41	30	10 08	67
50	35	33	19	72
52	33	34	24	74
54	30	36	30	77
56	26	38	36	80
58	23	40	43	84
60	5 19	43	10 52	88
S				

Lat.	Sunset	Twlt.	Moonset	Diff.
N				
°	h m	m	h m	m
70	17 10	61	25 08	*
68	17	56	24 38	150
66	22	52	24 16	121
64	27	48	23 59	107
62	30	45	45	98
60	34	42	33	91
58	37	40	23	86
56	39	38	14	82
54	42	36	06	79
52	44	34	23 00	75
50	46	32	22 53	73
45	51	30	40	67
40	55	28	29	63
35	17 58	26	19	60
30	18 01	24	22 11	57
20	06	23	21 57	52
10	11	21	45	48
0	15	21	33	45
10	20	21	22	40
20	25	22	21 10	36
30	31	24	20 56	32
35	35	26	48	29
40	38	28	39	26
45	43	30	28	22
50	49	33	16	17
52	51	34	10	14
54	54	36	20 03	12
56	18 57	38	19 56	09
58	19 01	41	48	05
60	19 04	44	19 39	01
S				

leaf) for each day. (It is customary to tear out the leaf at the end of the navigation day so the first page is always the current day.)

We have reprinted on pages 73 and 74 the entire leaf for March 4, 1949, the Greenwich A.M. side (0–12h) being on page 73 and the P.M. side (13–24h) on page 74.

You will note that the GHA and the declination of the sun are given in the first column for every 10 minutes of the day. We run down the column until we come to the first 10-minute interval *before* our GCT of 11h 14m 12s.

GREENWICH A. M. 1949 MARCH 4 (FRIDAY)

GCT	☉ SUN GHA	SUN Dec.	♈ GHA	VENUS—3.4 GHA	VENUS Dec.	JUPITER—1.5 GHA	JUPITER Dec.	SATURN 0.4 GHA	SATURN Dec.	☾ MOON GHA	MOON Dec.	☾ Par.
h m	° ′	° ′	° ′	° ′	° ′	° ′	° ′	° ′	° ′	° ′	° ′	
0 00	177 00	S 6 39	161 25	186 58	S11 58	225 38	S21 27	6 48	N12 27	135 42	N10 48	
10	179 30		163 56	189 28		228 08		9 18		138 08	50	
20	182 00		166 26	191 58		230 38		11 48		140 34	53	
30	184 [illegible] •	•	168 [illegible]	194 28 •	•	233 09 •	•	14 19 •	•	143 00 •	[illegible]	
40	[illegible]		[illegible]	[illegible]		235 39		[illegible]		[illegible]	[illegible]	
[illegible]	[illegible] 02		[illegible] 51	341 [illegible]				162 [illegible]			[illegible]	[illegible]
[illegible]0	334 32 •	•	319 21	344 22 •	•	2[illegible] 28 •	•	164 45 •	•	288 50 •	04	
40	337 02		321 52	346 52		25 59		167 16		291 15	06	Corr. HA ☾
50	339 32		324 22	349 22		28 29		169 46		293 41	08	
11 00	342 02	S 6 28	326 52	351 52	S11 46	30 59	S21 26	172 17	N12 27	296 07	N13 10	
10	344 32		329 23	354 22		33 30		174 47		298 33	13	m Int. ′ Corr.
20	347 02		331 53	356 52		36 00		177 18		300 59	15	
30	349 32 •	•	334 24	359 22 •	•	38 30 •	•	179 48 •	•	303 24 •	17	
40	352 02		336 54	1 52		41 01		182 19		305 50	19	0 0
50	354 32		339 25	4 22		43 31		184 49		308 16	21	5 +1
												10
12 00	357 02	S 6 27	341 55	6 52	S11 45	46 01	S21 26	187 19	N12 27	310 42	N13 23	

This is 11h 10m and so we jot down:

GCT 11h 10m 00s = 344°32′ GHA

At the same time, at one side of our worksheet, we jot down the declination of 6° 28S.

Now we must interpolate for the additional 4 minutes and 12 seconds of GHA from the 10-minute interval of 11h 10m to our GCT of 11h 14m 12s. We turn to the interpolation table on the inside front cover of the almanac (it is reprinted here on the opposite page). We find by this table that the additional GHA of 4 minutes and 12 seconds amounts to 1° 03′. This we add to our first figure:

	11h 10m 00s	=	344° 32′	
	4m 12s	=	1° 03′	
GCT	11h 14m 12s	=	345° 35′	GHA

Now we start the time diagram:

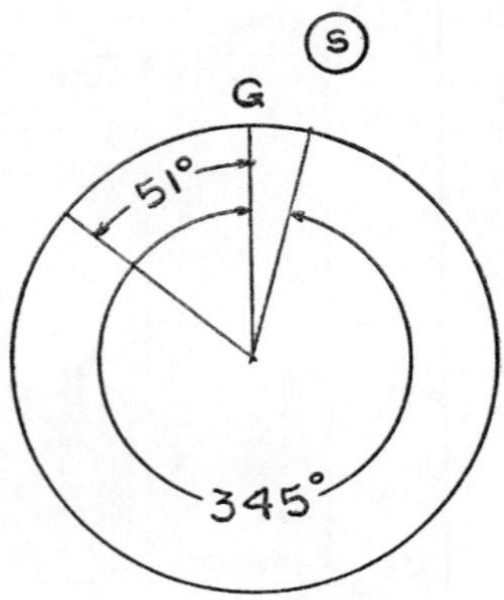

Our next step is to find the Local Hour Angle (LHA), or the distance from our meridian to the sun's meridian.

In modern systems we short-cut a lot of bookkeeping by not using the exact dead-reckoning position for determining the LHA, but by *assuming* a near-by longitude that will give us a whole degree of LHA. (Our dead-reckoning position is just a guess anyway; so while we are about it we also assume the nearest full degree of latitude.)

INTERPOLATION OF GHA

SUN, PLANETS, ♈

Int. (m s)	Corr. (° ′)	Int. (m s)	Corr. (° ′)	Int. (m s)	Corr. (° ′)
00 00	0 00	03 17	0 50	06 37	1 40
01	0 01	21	0 51	41	1 41
05	0 02	25	0 52	45	1 42
09	0 03	29	0 53	49	1 43
13	0 04	33	0 54	53	1 44
17	0 05	37	0 55	57	1 45
21	0 06	41	0 56	07 01	1 46
25	0 07	45	0 57	05	1 47
29	0 08	49	0 58	09	1 48
33	0 09	53	0 59	13	1 49
37	0 10	57	1 00	17	1 50
41	0 11	04 01	1 01	21	1 51
45	0 12	05	1 02	25	1 52
49	0 13	09	1 03	29	1 53
53	0 14	13	1 04	33	1 54
57	0 15	17	1 05	37	1 55
01 01	0 16	21	1 06	41	1 56
05	0 17	25	1 07	45	1 57
09	0 18	29	1 08	49	1 58
13	0 19	33	1 09	53	1 59
17	0 20	37	1 10	57	2 00
21	0 21	41	1 11	08 01	2 01
25	0 22	45	1 12	05	2 02
29	0 23	49	1 13	09	2 03
33	0 24	53	1 14	13	2 04
37	0 25	57	1 15	17	2 05
41	0 26	05 01	1 16	21	2 06
45	0 27	05	1 17	25	2 07
49	0 28	09	1 18	29	2 08
53	0 29	13	1 19	33	2 09
57	0 30	17	1 20	37	2 10
02 01	0 31	21	1 21	41	2 11
05	0 32	25	1 22	45	2 12
09	0 33	29	1 23	49	2 13
13	0 34	33	1 24	53	2 14
17	0 35	37	1 25	57	2 15
21	0 36	41	1 26	09 01	2 16
25	0 37	45	1 27	05	2 17
29	0 38	49	1 28	09	2 18
33	0 39	53	1 29	13	2 19
37	0 40	57	1 30	17	2 20
41	0 41	06 01	1 31	21	2 21
45	0 42	05	1 32	25	2 22
49	0 43	09	1 33	29	2 23
53	0 44	13	1 34	33	2 24
57	0 45	17	1 35	37	2 25
03 01	0 46	21	1 36	41	2 26
05	0 47	25	1 37	45	2 27
09	0 48	29	1 38	49	2 28
13	0 49	33	1 39	53	2 29
17	0 50	37	1 40	57	2 30
21		41		10 00	

MOON

Int. (m s)	Corr. (° ′)	Int. (m s)	Corr. (° ′)	Int. (m s)	Corr. (° ′)
00 00	0 00	03 20	0 49	06 39	1 37
02	0 01	24	0 50	43	1 38
06	0 02	29	0 51	47	1 39
10	0 03	33	0 52	52	1 40
14	0 04	37	0 53	56	1 41
18	0 05	41	0 54	07 00	1 42
22	0 06	45	0 55	04	1 43
26	0 07	49	0 56	08	1 44
31	0 08	53	0 57	12	1 45
35	0 09	58	0 58	16	1 46
39	0 10	04 02	0 59	20	1 47
43	0 11	06	1 00	25	1 48
47	0 12	10	1 01	29	1 49
51	0 13	14	1 02	33	1 50
55	0 14	18	1 03	37	1 51
01 00	0 15	22	1 04	41	1 52
04	0 16	27	1 05	45	1 53
08	0 17	31	1 06	49	1 54
12	0 18	35	1 07	54	1 55
16	0 19	39	1 08	58	1 56
20	0 20	43	1 09	08 02	1 57
24	0 21	47	1 10	06	1 58
29	0 22	51	1 11	10	1 59
33	0 23	56	1 12	14	2 00
37	0 24	05 00	1 13	18	2 01
41	0 25	04	1 14	23	2 02
45	0 26	08	1 15	27	2 03
49	0 27	12	1 16	31	2 04
53	0 28	16	1 17	35	2 05
58	0 29	20	1 18	39	2 06
02 02	0 30	25	1 19	43	2 07
06	0 31	29	1 20	47	2 08
10	0 32	33	1 21	52	2 09
14	0 33	37	1 22	56	2 10
18	0 34	41	1 23	09 00	2 11
22	0 35	45	1 24	04	2 12
26	0 36	49	1 25	08	2 13
31	0 37	54	1 26	12	2 14
35	0 38	58	1 27	16	2 15
39	0 39	06 02	1 28	21	2 16
43	0 40	06	1 29	25	2 17
47	0 41	10	1 30	29	2 18
51	0 42	14	1 31	33	2 19
55	0 43	18	1 32	37	2 20
03 00	0 44	23	1 33	41	2 21
04	0 45	27	1 34	45	2 22
08	0 46	31	1 35	50	2 23
12	0 47	35	1 36	54	2 24
16	0 48	39	1 37	58	2 25
20	0 49	43		10 00	
24					

Correction to be added to GHA for interval of GCT

In this case we assume a longitude of 51 35W and a latitude of 31N.

GHA	345°35′
Assumed Longitude	51°35′
LHA	294°

And this LHA being greater than 180°, we subtract it from 360° to find the LHA of 66°.

We put this in our time diagram:

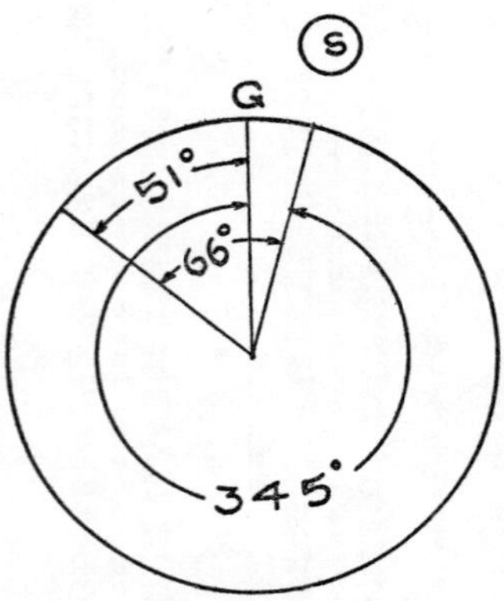

Now consider what has happened:

We have spotted the sun's position exactly. It is directly above 6 28S and 345 35W (or 14 25E) and its meridian is approximately 66° to the east of us.

We are through with the almanac now and are ready to ask the tables the $64 question: "If we were at the assumed position of 31N and 51 35W at 11h 14m 12s on March 4, 1949, what should our sextant read on a sun sight?"

This question can be answered by any number of navigation tables, several printed by the government and scores printed privately. Gluttons for punishment can even work out the problem by logarithms, but as we believe in taking the easiest way we are going to let the mathematicians do the work for us.

The *Tables of Computed Altitude and Azimuth*, better known as *H.O. 214*, are divided into six volumes, each covering 10° of latitude (600 miles) for either north or south of the equator. We pick up Volume IV (30° to 39°) and turn to the section marked for our latitude of 31N.

On one side of the page we find tables for use when the latitude is the *same name* as the declination (north and north and south and south); on the other side when the names are *contrary*—when one is north and the other is south.

The columns are for every half degree of declination. We turn the pages until we come to the page that has the nearest half degree of declination *below* the one we want. This is the column for 6°.

We run our finger down this column until we find the LHA (marked simply HA in the tables) for our own of 66°.

We jot down the first figure (17°02′) which is the altitude, the second figure (57) which is a multiplying factor for interpolation

(Δd), and the last figure (108°) which is the azimuth. (The fraction after this figure is generally disregarded.)

DECLINATION CONTRARY NAME TO LATITUDE — 31 — Lat. 31°

H.A.	4° 00′ Alt.	Δd Δt	Az.	4° 30′ Alt.	Δd Δt	Az.	5° 00′ Alt.	Δd Δt	Az.	5° 30′ Alt.	Δd Δt	Az.	6° 00′ Alt.	Δd Δt	Az.	6° 30′ Alt.	Δd Δt	Az.	7° 00′ Alt.	Δd Δt	Az.	7° 30′ Alt.	Δd Δt	Az.	H.A.
°	° ′		°	° ′		°	° ′		°	° ′		°	° ′		°	° ′		°	° ′		°	° ′		°	°
00	55 00.0	1.0 01	180.0	54 30.0	1.0 01	180.0	54 00.0	1.0 01	180.0	53 30.0	1.0 01	180.0	53 00.0	1.0 01	180.0	52 30.0	1.0 01	180.0	52 00.0	1.0 01	180.0	51 30.0	1.0 01	180.0	00
1	54 59.2	1.0 04	178.3	54 29.2	1.0 04	178.3	53 59.3	1.0 04	178.3	53 29.2	1.0 04	178.3	52 59.3	1.0 04	178.4	52 29.3	1.0 04	178.4	51 59.3	1.0 04	178.4	51 29.3	1.0 03	178.4	1
2	54 56.9	1.0 06	176.5	54 26.9	1.0 06	176.5	53 57.0	1.0 06	176.6	53 27.0	1.0 06	176.6	52 57.0	1.0 06	176.7	52 27.1	1.0 06	176.7	51 57.1	1.0 06	176.8	51 27.2	1.0 06	176.8	2
3	54 53.0	99 09	174.8	54 23.1	99 09	174.8	53 53.3	99 09	174.9	53 23.2	99 09	175.0	52 53.4	1.0 09	175.1	52 23.4	1.0 08	175.1	51 53.5	1.0 08	175.2	51 23.6	1.0 08	175.2	3
4	54 47.6	99 11	173.1	54 17.7	99 11	173.1	53 47.9	99 11	173.2	53 17.9	99 11	173.3	52 48.2	99 11	173.4	52 18.3	99 11	173.5	51 48.5	99 11	173.6	51 18.6	99 11	173.6	4
05	54 40.7	99 14	171.4	54 10.8	99 14	171.5	53 41.1	99 14	171.6	53 11.3	99 14	171.7	52 41.6	99 13	171.8	52 11.8	99 13	171.9	51 42.0	99 13	172.0	51 12.2	99 13	172.1	05
6	54 32.1	99 16	169.6	54 02.4	99 16	169.7	53 32.8	99 16	169.9	53 03.1	99 16	170.0	52 33.5	99 16	170.2	52 03.8	99 16	170.3	51 34.1	99 15	170.4	51 04.4	99 15	170.5	6
7	54 22.2	98 19	168.0	53 52.6	98 19	168.1	53 23.1	98 19	168.3	52 53.5	98 18	168.4	52 24.0	98 18	168.5	51 54.4	98 18	168.6	51 24.9	99 18	168.8	50 55.2	99 17	168.9	7
8	54 10.7	98 21	166.3	53 41.3	98 21	166.4	53 11.9	98 21	166.6	52 42.4	98 21	166.7	52 13.1	98 20	166.9	51 43.6	98 20	167.1	51 14.2	98 20	167.3	50 44.7	98 20	167.4	8
9	53 57.8	97 24	164.6	53 28.5	97 24	164.8	52 59.3	97 23	165.0	52 30.0	97 23	165.2	52 00.8	98 23	165.4	51 31.4	98 22	165.5	51 02.1	98 22	165.7	50 32.8	98 22	165.8	9
10	53 43.4	97 26	163.0	53 14.3	97 26	163.2	52 45.3	97 26	163.4	52 16.1	97 25	163.6	51 47.0	97 25	163.8	51 17.9	97 25	164.0	50 48.7	97 24	164.2	50 19.6	97 24	164.3	10
1	53 27.7	96 29	161.4	52 58.7	96 28	161.6	52 29.9	96 28	161.8	52 00.9	96 27	162.0	51 32.0	96 27	162.2	51 03.1	96 27	162.4	50 34.1	97 27	162.7	50 05.1	97 26	162.9	1
2	53 10.5	96 31	159.8	52 41.8	96 30	160.0	52 13.2	96 30	160.3	51 44.4	96 30	160.5	51 15.7	96 29	160.7	50 46.9	96 29	160.9	50 18.1	96 29	161.2	49 49.3	96 28	161.4	2
3	52 52.1	95 33	158.2	52 23.6	95 33	158.4	51 55.2	95 32	158.7	51 26.6	95 32	158.9	50 58.1	95 32	159.2	50 29.5	95 31	159.4	50 00.9	95 31	159.7	49 32.2	95 30	159.9	3
4	52 32.3	94 35	156.6	52 04.0	94 35	156.9	51 35.8	94 34	157.2	51 07.5	94 34	157.4	50 39.1	95 33	157.7	50 10.8	95 33	157.9	49 42.4	95 33	158.2	49 13.9	95 32	158.4	4
15	52 11.3	93 37	155.1	51 43.2	93 37	155.4	51 15.2	93 36	155.7	50 47.1	93 36	155.9	50 19.0	94 35	156.2	49 50.9	94 35	156.4	49 22.7	94 35	156.7	48 54.5	94 34	157.0	15
6	51 49.0	92 39	153.6	51 21.2	92 39	153.9	50 53.5	93 38	154.2	50 25.6	93 38	154.4	49 57.7	93 37	154.8	49 29.8	93 37	155.0	49 01.8	93 37	155.3	48 33.8	93 36	155.6	6
7	51 25.6	91 41	152.1	50 58.0	91 41	152.4	50 30.5	92 40	152.7	50 02.8	92 40	153.0	49 35.2	92 39	153.3	49 07.5	92 39	153.6	48 39.8	92 39	153.9	48 12.0	92 38	154.2	7
8	51 00.9	90 43	150.7	50 33.6	90 42	151.0	50 06.4	91 42	151.3	49 38.9	91 41	151.6	49 11.6	91 41	151.9	48 44.1	91 41	152.2	48 16.6	92 40	152.6	47 49.1	92 40	152.8	8
9	50 35.1	90 45	149.2	50 08.1	90 44	149.6	49 41.1	90 44	149.9	49 14.0	90 43	150.2	48 46.9	91 43	150.6	48 19.6	91 42	150.9	47 52.4	91 42	151.2	47 25.1	91 42	151.5	9
20	50 08.3	89 47	147.8	49 41.5	89 46	148.1	49 14.8	89 46	148.5	48 47.9	89 45	148.8	48 21.0	90 45	149.2	47 54.1	90 44	149.5	47 27.1	90 44	149.9	47 00.0	90 43	150.2	20
1	49 40.3	88 48	146.5	49 13.9	88 48	146.8	48 47.3	89 47	147.2	48 20.8	89 47	147.5	47 54.2	89 46	147.9	47 27.5	89 46	148.3	47 00.8	89 45	148.6	46 33.9	89 45	148.9	1
2	49 11.5	87 50	145.1	48 45.3	87 49	145.5	48 19.1	88 49	145.9	47 52.7	88 48	146.2	47 26.4	88 48	146.6	46 59.9	88 47	146.9	46 33.5	88 47	147.3	46 06.9	88 47	147.6	2
3	48 41.6	86 51	143.8	48 15.7	86 51	144.2	47 49.8	87 51	144.6	47 23.7	87 50	[illegible]	[illegible]	[illegible]	[illegible]	46 31.4	87 49	145.6	[illegible]	87 49	146.0	45 38.8	[illegible]	[illegible]	[illegible]
[illegible]	[illegible]	[illegible]	[illegible]	[illegible]	[illegible]	142.9	47 19.[illegible]	[illegible]	[illegible]	[illegible]	[illegible]	[illegible]	[illegible]	[illegible]	[illegible]	[illegible]	[illegible]	[illegible]	[illegible]	[illegible]	144.8	[illegible]	[illegible]	[illegible]	[illegible]
[illegible]	[illegible]	[illegible]	[illegible]	[illegible]	[illegible]	[illegible]	[illegible]	[illegible]	[illegible]	[illegible]	[illegible]	118.3	29 36.7	66 75	118.8	[illegible]	[illegible]	[illegible]	[illegible]	[illegible]	[illegible]	[illegible]	66 74	120.1	50
1	30 08.8	64 77	116.3	29 49.5	64 77	[illegible]	[illegible]	64 76	117.2	29 10.9	64 76	117.6	28 51.5	65 76	118.1	28 32.0	65 76	118.5	28 12.4	[illegible]	[illegible]	27 52.7	66 75	119.3	1
2	29 22.5	63 77	115.6	29 03.5	63 77	116.0	28 44.4	64 77	116.5	28 25.2	64 77	116.9	28 06.0	64 76	117.3	27 46.6	64 76	117.7	27 27.2	65 76	118.2	27 07.7	65 75	118.6	2
3	28 36.0	63 78	114.9	28 17.1	63 78	115.3	27 58.2	63 77	115.7	27 39.2	63 77	116.1	27 20.1	64 77	116.6	27 01.0	64 77	117.0	26 41.7	64 76	117.5	26 22.4	64 76	117.9	3
4	27 49.1	62 78	114.1	27 30.5	62 78	114.5	27 11.8	63 78	115.0	26 52.9	63 77	115.4	26 34.0	63 77	115.9	26 15.0	63 77	116.3	25 55.9	64 77	116.8	25 36.8	64 76	117.2	4
55	27 02.1	62 79	113.4	26 43.6	62 79	113.8	26 25.0	62 78	114.3	26 06.4	62 78	114.7	25 47.6	63 78	115.2	25 28.8	63 77	115.6	25 09.9	63 77	116.1	24 50.9	63 77	116.5	55
6	26 14.8	61 79	112.8	25 56.4	61 79	113.2	25 38.1	62 79	113.6	25 19.5	62 78	114.0	25 00.9	62 78	114.5	24 42.3	62 78	114.9	24 23.6	63 78	115.4	24 04.7	63 77	115.8	6
7	25 27.3	61 80	112.1	25 09.0	61 79	112.5	24 50.8	61 79	113.0	24 32.5	61 79	113.4	24 14.1	62 79	113.8	23 55.5	62 78	114.2	23 37.0	62 78	114.7	23 18.3	62 78	115.1	7
8	24 39.5	60 80	111.4	24 21.4	60 80	111.8	24 03.4	61 79	112.3	23 45.2	61 79	112.7	23 26.9	61 79	113.2	23 08.5	61 79	113.6	22 50.1	62 78	114.0	22 31.6	62 78	114.4	8
9	23 51.5	60 80	110.8	23 33.6	60 80	111.2	23 15.7	60 80	111.7	22 57.6	60 80	112.1	22 39.5	61 79	112.5	22 21.3	61 79	112.9	22 03.0	61 79	113.4	21 44.7	61 79	113.8	9
60	23 03.3	59 81	110.1	22 45.5	59 80	110.5	22 27.7	60 80	111.0	22 09.8	60 80	111.4	21 51.8	60 80	111.9	21 33.8	60 79	112.3	21 15.6	61 79	112.7	20 57.5	61 79	113.1	60
1	22 14.9	59 81	109.5	21 57.3	59 81	109.9	21 39.6	59 80	110.4	21 21.8	59 80	110.8	21 04.0	60 80	111.2	20 46.1	60 80	111.6	20 28.1	60 79	112.1	20 10.1	60 79	112.5	1
2	21 26.4	58 81	108.9	21 08.9	58 81	109.3	20 51.2	59 81	109.7	20 33.7	59 81	110.1	20 16.0	59 80	110.6	19 58.2	59 80	111.0	19 40.4	60 80	111.5	19 22.5	60 80	111.9	2
3	20 37.7	58 82	108.3	20 20.2	58 81	108.7	20 02.8	58 81	109.1	19 45.3	58 81	109.5	19 27.7	59 81	110.0	19 10.1	59 80	110.4	18 52.4	59 80	110.8	18 34.7	59 80	111.1	3
4	19 48.7	58 82	107.6	19 31.4	58 82	108.0	19 14.1	58 81	108.5	18 56.7	58 81	108.9	18 39.3	58 81	109.4	18 21.8	58 81	109.8	18 04.2	59 80	110.2	17 46.6	59 80	110.6	4
65	18 59.6	57 82	107.0	18 42.4	57 82	107.4	18 25.3	57 82	107.9	18 08.0	57 81	108.3	17 50.7	58 81	108.8	17 33.3	58 81	109.2	17 15.9	58 81	109.6	16 58.4	58 81	110.0	65
6	18 10.3	57 82	106.4	17 53.3	57 82	106.8	17 36.3	57 82	107.3	17 19.1	57 82	107.7	17 02.0	57 82	108.2	16 44.5	57 81	108.6	16 27.4	58 81	109.0	16 10.0	58 81	109.4	6
7	17 20.9	56 82	105.8	17 04.0	56 82	106.2	16 47.1	57 82	106.7	16 30.0	57 82	107.1	16 13.0	57 82	107.6	15 55.8	57 82	108.0	15 38.7	57 81	108.4	15 21.4	57 81	108.8	7
8	16 31.4	56 83	105.3	16 14.5	56 82	105.7	15 57.7	56 82	106.1	15 40.8	56 82	106.5	15 23.9	57 82	107.0	15 06.8	57 82	107.4	14 49.8	57 82	107.8	14 32.7	57 82	108.2	8
9	15 41.7	56 83	104.7	15 25.0	56 83	105.1	15 08.2	56 83	105.5	14 51.4	56 82	105.9	14 34.5	56 82	106.4	14 17.7	57 82	106.8	14 00.7	57 82	107.3	13 43.7	57 82	107.7	9
70	14 51.9	55 83	104.1	14 35.2	56 83	104.5	14 18.6	56 83	105.0	14 01.9	56 83	105.4	13 45.1	56 82	105.8	13 28.4	56 82	106.2	13 11.6	56 82	106.7	12 54.6	56 82	107.1	70
1	14 02.0	55 83	103.5	13 45.4	55 83	103.9	13 28.9	55 83	104.4	13 12.3	55 83	104.8	12 55.6	56 83	105.3	12 38.9	56 83	105.7	12 22.1	56 82	106.1	12 05.4	56 82	106.5	1
2	13 11.9	55 84	103.0	12 55.4	55 83	103.4	12 39.0	55 83	103.8	12 22.5	55 83	104.2	12 05.9	55 83	104.7	11 49.3	55 83	105.1	11 32.7	55 83	105.5	11 16.0	55 82	105.9	2
3	12 21.7	55 84	102.4	12 05.3	55 84	102.8	11 49.0	54 83	103.3	11 32.6	54 83	103.7	11 16.1	55 83	104.1	10 59.6	55 83	104.5	10 43.1	55 83	105.0	10 26.5	55 83	105.4	3
4	11 31.4	54 84	101.9	11 15.1	54 84	102.3	10 58.9	54 84	102.7	10 42.6	54 84	103.1	10 26.2	55 83	103.6	10 09.8	55 83	104.0	9 53.4	55 83	104.4	9 36.9	55 83	104.8	4
75	10 41.1	54 84	101.3	10 24.8	54 84	101.7	10 08.7	54 84	102.2	9 52.4	54 84	102.6	9 36.2	54 84	103.0	9 19.8	54 83	103.4	9 03.5	55 83	103.9	8 47.1	55 83	104.3	75
6	9 50.6	54 84	100.8	9 34.4	54 84	101.2	9 18.4	54 84	101.6	9 02.2	54 84	102.0	8 46.0	54 84	102.5	8 29.7	54 84	102.9	8 13.5	54 83	103.3	7 57.2	54 83	103.7	6
7	9 00.0	54 84	100.2	8 43.9	54 84	100.6	8 27.9	54 84	101.1	8 11.8	54 84	101.5	7 55.7	54 84	101.9	7 39.5	54 84	102.3	7 23.4	54 84	102.8	7 07.2	54 83	103.2	7
8	8 09.3	53 84	99.7	7 53.4	53 84	100.1	7 37.4	53 84	100.5	7 21.4	53 84	100.9	7 05.3	54 84	101.4	6 49.3	54 84	101.8	6 33.2	54 84	102.2	6 17.1	54 84	102.6	8
9	7 18.6	53 85	99.2	7 02.7	53 85	99.6	6 46.8	53 84	100.0	6 30.9	53 84	100.4	6 14.9	53 84	100.9	5 58.9	53 84	101.3	5 42.9	53 84	101.7	5 26.8	54 84	102.1	9
80	6 27.8	53 85	98.6	6 11.9	53 85	99.0	5 56.1	53 85	99.5	5 40.2	53 84	99.9	5 24.3	53 84	100.3	5 08.4	53 84	100.7							80
1	5 36.9	53 85	98.1	5 21.1	53 85	98.5	5 05.3	53 85	99.0																1

The altitude must still be corrected for the difference in the declination between 6° and the 6°28′ given us in the almanac. In other words, we must multiply the factor of 57 times the 28′ of remaining declination. The factor "57" is nothing more than 57/100 of a minute, but in the inside back cover of the volume is a convenient multiplication table.

The question of whether we add or subtract this correction is decided by glancing at the adjoining columns. If you will look at the reprint opposite, you will see that the altitude is *decreasing,* as the declination *increases*—in other words, the column to the right which is for 6°30′ declination has less altitude than the 6° column we are using.

So we multiply our factor of 57 times the 28′ for a correction of 16′, then subtract like this:

Alt.	17°02′
Corr.	—16′
Hc	16°46′

The corrected altitude is called the *Computed Altitude (Hc).*

There is the answer from the tables. It says to us:

"If you were at 31N, 51 35W at 11h 14m 12s on March 4, 1949, the altitude of the sun would be 16°46′ and its azimuth 108°."

Now we are ready to plot our line of position.

BEFORE, however, we start our plotting we return to the observed altitude we found with the sextant and compare it with the computed altitude. The Ho was 16°51′; the Hc 16°46′. We find the difference:

Ho	16°51′	
Hc	16°46′	
Difference	5′	(This is called the *intercept*)

That means that we are on a line of position 5′ from the line of position that cuts the assumed position. And as the observed sight is greater than the computed sight the intercept is *toward* the sun, that is, closer to the sun than the assumed line of position.

And now we plot it.

First we find the assumed position (31N, 51 35W) on the plotting sheet and mark it with a tiny *x*. Then with the help of the protractor we draw the azimuth line toward the sun. We do this just like we drew the bearing lines in alongshore navigation except we start it from our assumed position and draw it far enough along to cover our intercept.

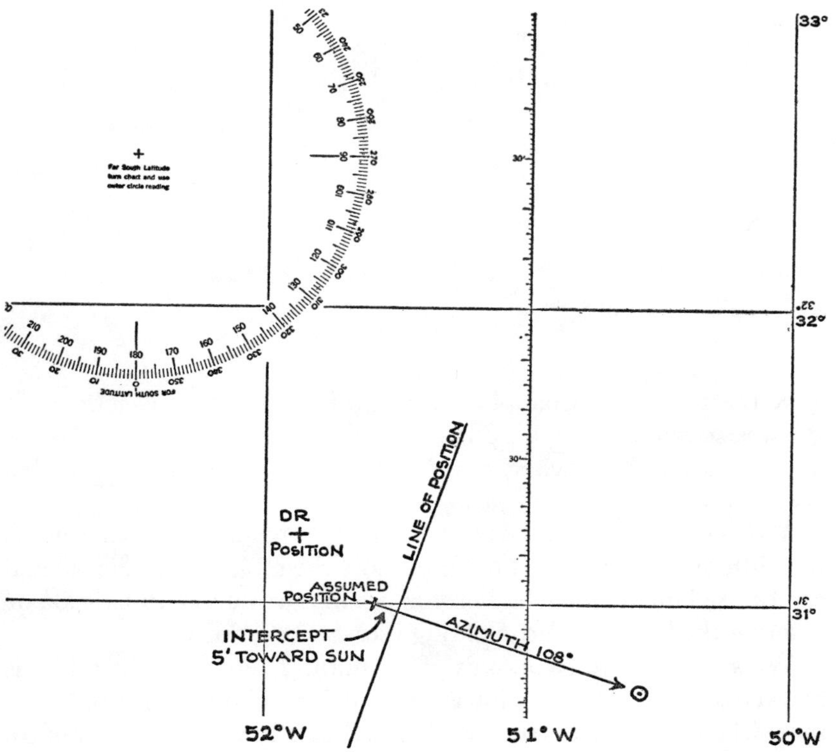

Now we take our dividers and by our latitude scale measure the intercept of 5′ or 5 miles from the assumed position along the azimuth line toward the sun. At that point we draw our line of position at right angles to the azimuth line.

We are on that line.

IN the preceding example we applied the *azimuth* exactly as it was stated in the tables. It is not always that this can be done. This is another case, where for the sake of having condensed tables, we must do a little more figuring.

You will note that in the tables there is no mention of either north or south or east or west. That is because the tables are universal and can be used no matter whether you are in north or south latitude or whether the body you are sighting is east or west of you.

We say there are two kinds of azimuth. The one in the tables is marked Z. The one we plot is marked *Zn.* The two are only the same when we are in north latitude and the body we sight is east of us.

Azimuth Z as given in the tables is measured from the *nearest* pole, instead of from the North Pole, as we do on the compass. Besides that it only runs to 180° on the side you are pointing your sextant. But it is easier pictured than described. Here is a comprehensive diagram of the two azimuths, the outer circle also being the compass circle, and for the sake of argument, the Z being given as 100°.

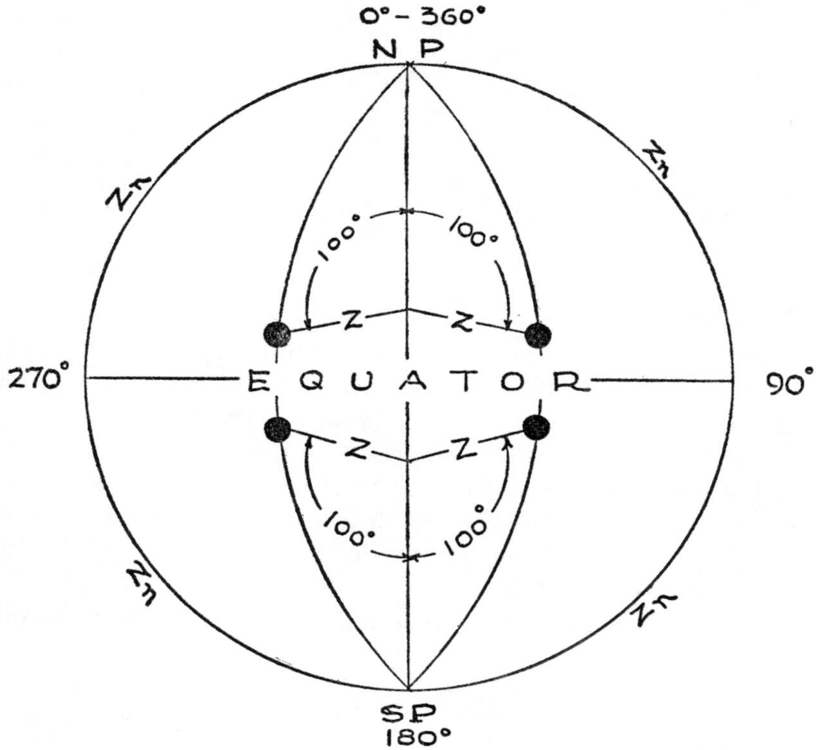

See that only in the northeast quarter are Z and Zn the same. In the northwest quarter (which would have been the case in the preceding example had the sight been taken in the afternoon), to translate Z to Zn we must subtract it from 360°. In the southeast quarter we subtract it from 180°, and in the southwest quarter we add 180°.

Here is another case in which a rule can be memorized but a diagram is better. When in doubt—to be cautious *always* do it—draw a diagram something like the one above and figure out in which quarter you are working and reason out what you must do.

TAKING sights on the planets is as easy as on the sun. In fact it is easier, for the planets do not have to be corrected for semi-diameter. The navigation planets are Venus, Mars, Jupiter and Saturn, and those visible are listed in the Air Almanac.

After you have corrected your sextant reading for I.C., dip, and refraction you enter the almanac in the same manner that you did for the sun sight, taking the GHA of the planet from near-by the sun column. Then proceed to work out the sight in the same manner as you do a sun sight.

For years navigators shuddered at the thought of working a moon

sight, and many ships were lost because of this distaste and the possibility of error in the complicated figuring necessary. As late as 1920, the author of a famous textbook on navigation wrote: "For purposes of navigation the moon is a nuisance." But today, thanks to the Air Almanac, a moon sight is worked almost as easily as a sun sight. Only one additional correction is made.

The moon sight is worked exactly like a sun sight except that you enter the moon table and interpolate by the moon interpolation table which adjoins the other interpolation table on the inside cover of the almanac. In correcting your sextant altitude, you must add in the correction for parallax which is found in the last column of the daily A.M. page. Then work out your sight as you do with the sun.

It is a happy day for the navigator when the moon is visible in the daytime, for then he can get fixes by simultaneous sights of the sun and moon.

Along the margin of each daily A.M. page in the Air Almanac is an ingenious strip that shows the position that day of the planets, moon, and four prominent stars relative to the sun. The sun being in the center of each strip, the navigator, at a glance, can tell the approximate position of the planets in the skies and what to expect in later hours.

IN working a star sight you must add in one more factor, but as you leave out the correction for semi-diameter the difference in time and effort is slight.

The reason for this added factor is not in the nature of the star sight but once again for the sake of condensation of tables. There are 55 navigation stars scattered over the heavens and 55 GHA columns in the Air Almanac would make the book so bulky it would be useless afloat.

Fortunately the stars move barely at all from their nightly positions—they are sometimes called fixed stars—and so the almanac can disregard any change in GHA or declination of the stars relative to each other.

As the geographers decided to start measuring the earth from Greenwich, so the astronomers, many years ago, decided to start their measurements from a point in the heavens called *The First Point of Aries,* where the sun crossed the equator on its northern movement in the spring. It is also called the *Vernal Equinox,* but today most navigators refer to it simply as *Aries* and so will we.

From this point all stars are measured westward for 360°, just as GHA is measured westward from Greenwich for the same number of degrees.

This measurement is called the *Sidereal Hour Angle* (sidereal meaning, "of the stars"). It is abbreviated SHA and its symbol is ♈. The SHA of all navigation stars is found on the inside back cover of the Air Almanac and alongside is found the star's declination. On each daily page of the Air Almanac next to the sun column will be found the GHA of Aries.

To find the GHA of a star, merely add the GHA of Aries to the SHA of the star, subtracting 360° whenever the total runs over that figure.

Let us say that your assumed longitude was 48W, the SHA of a star 188°, and the GHA of Aries 88°. Your time diagram would look like this:

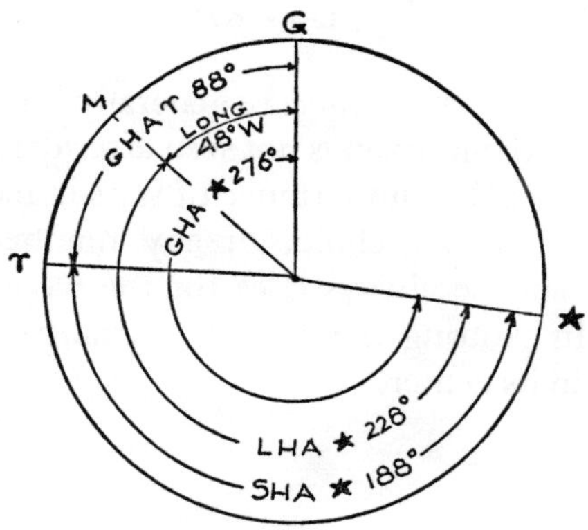

In other words the LHA of the star would be 228° to the west of the assumed position, or (360° — 228°) 132° to the east.

A time diagram is most important in star sights and the position of Aries should always be drawn in. It is also a good idea to draw in the position of the sun just to make sure it hasn't passed the 180° meridian so that another navigation day has begun. One of the most frequent errors in star sights is entering the wrong navigation day.

Here are three more time diagrams:

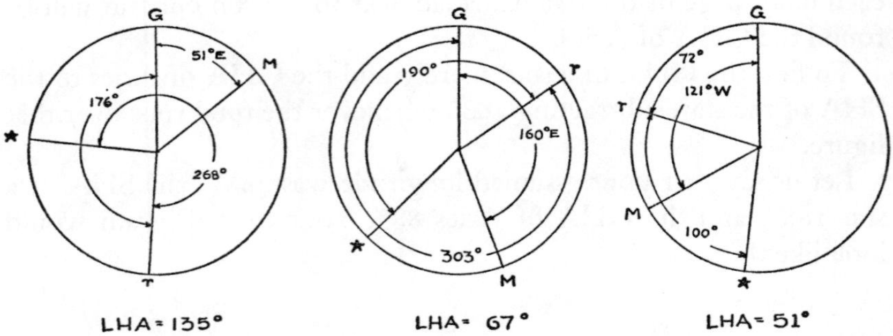

In marine navigation, star sights are generally limited to dawn and evening twilight, as the horizon is not seen after dark except on very bright moonlit nights. The importance of stars in navigation is obvious: the navigator has his choice of any number of stars for a simultaneous fix, and he always tries for the navigation jackpot—a three-star fix. In plotting this he gets a triangle and he fixes his position as being in its center.

THE best way to learn the stars is to go out and look at them. Any sort of star chart will give the names and location of the navigation stars—the chart in the back of the Air Almanac is excellent—or a friend who knows them can point them out to you.

The important thing to remember is that *you* are the one who must know them, and any method of locating them must be convenient and sure in *your* mind. Everyone has a different mental pattern of the heavens, and with a little imagination you can make your own mental picture that will fix the position of the principal stars indelibly in your memory.

In north latitudes, knowledge of the position of the Big Dipper is sufficient to locate the navigation stars; south of the equator the Southern Cross will serve the same purpose. Start from either one with your chart, pick out the brightest stars—they are sure to be navigation stars—and learn their names. Then figure out a system for finding them again.

Don't be confused by trying to see the traditional figures of the constellation—the Lion, the Eagle, the Archer, etc. Many of the constellations have changed shape in the untold centuries since they were first named; many of them were named not because of resemblance, but in honor of some religious event or character that had to do with the names.

The planets, being members of our solar system, wander through the heavens and are often mistaken for stars. Use the marginal strip on the daily page of the Air Almanac to locate the planets, and before you shoot a star sight be sure they are safely accounted for.

Under general conditions a planet never twinkles and all stars do.

THE most useful single star in navigation is Polaris, the Pole Star. When visible, with a single simple correction it will give you latitude or a horizontal line of position without use of the navigation tables.

As Polaris is never more than one degree from being exactly above the North Pole, its altitude, corrected for its slight movement around the pole, is always your latitude. At the pole itself, its altitude would be approximately 90°, and on the equator, if it were visible, its altitude would be zero.

For centuries it has been used by mariners, many of whom observed it without a sextant and could only estimate its altitude. The Scandinavians probably used it in the first voyage to America, and it was Columbus' most reliable aid.

On the back of the star chart in the Air Almanac is a table of correction for Polaris. To use it you simply determine the LHA of Aries (♈) as you do in a regular star sight (you need not worry about minutes of angle; the nearest whole degree is enough), and apply this correction to your observed altitude. That will be your latitude, and you plot it as an east-west line of position. The practiced navigator, working for speed and the least work, will shoot Polaris and a planet for a fix or include Polaris in a three-star fix.

Two stars of the Big Dipper (called the "Plough," in England) point to Polaris, like this:

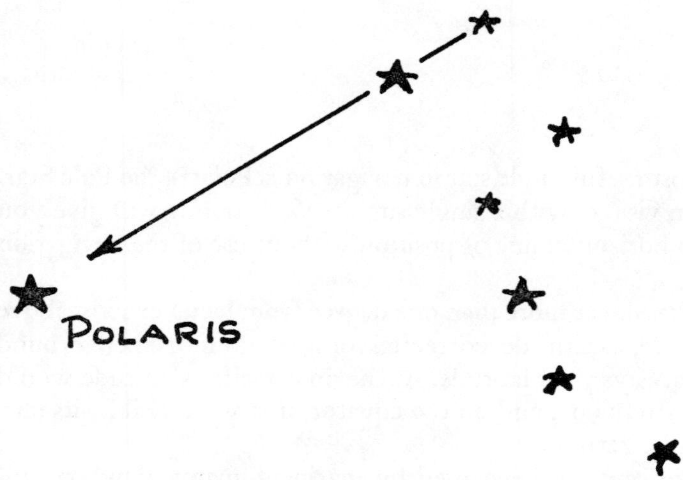

THE "POINTERS" OF THE BIG DIPPER POINT TO POLARIS

Polaris is about the *magnitude* or brightness of the last star in the handle of the dipper.

AS we pointed out before, every heavenly body has two motions —vertical and horizontal. That is, it moves north and south, changing its declination, and from east to west, changing its hour angle. For that reason we must use navigation tables like H.O. 214 to determine our line of position.

There are two times, however, when the navigation tables can be dispensed with. The first time we have just discussed in the Polaris sight. The second time is when the sun or star or planet or moon is on your meridian. When that happens you have the object cornered, and all you have to do is to determine its north-south movement, or declination, to get a line of position.

This is the basis of the noon latitude sight, sometimes called the noon meridian sight, one of the oldest and certainly the most widely used sight in navigation. For hundreds of years this sight and the Polaris sight were *all* the celestial navigation that existed. Still, America was discovered and colonized and the English mariners sailed around the globe by these two worthy sights, and today there are thousands of seasoned mariners who navigate up and down the coast with nothing else.

The only information needed in the noon latitude sight is the declination of the sun.

Let us say the sun's declination is 18°N, like this:

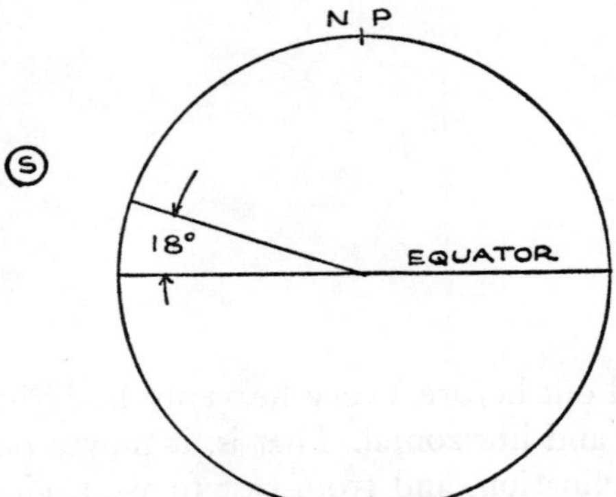

And you are somewhere north of the sun, like this:

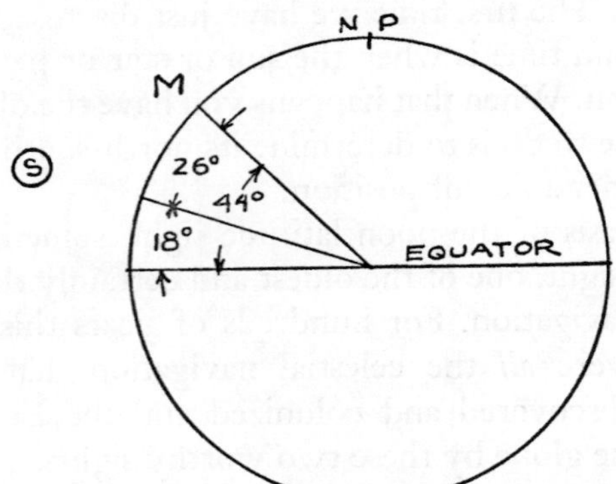

You take a sun sight when the sun is on the meridian and you get a corrected reading, say of 64°. Now think a moment.

If the sun were directly over your head, the *zenith*, the sextant would read 90°. Therefore, as the earth is a globe and the dome of the heavens is a half globe, the global distance the sun is from your zenith is the sextant reading subtracted from 90°. This is known as *zenith distance.*

In this case the zenith distance is 90° — 64°, or 26°.

Now, if the sun's declination is 18°N, or it is 18° north of the equator, and you are 26° north of the sun, then you must be 18° + 26°, or 44° north of the equator.

That is your latitude, or your east-west line of position.

Naturally there are variations of this method. There is the case when the sun is south of the equator and you are north of it, when you are south of the equator, when the sun is north of you, etc.

Once again, however, we tell you not to memorize any rule but to draw a diagram and *see* what's happening.

Here is a diagram when the sun is south of the equator and you are in north latitude.

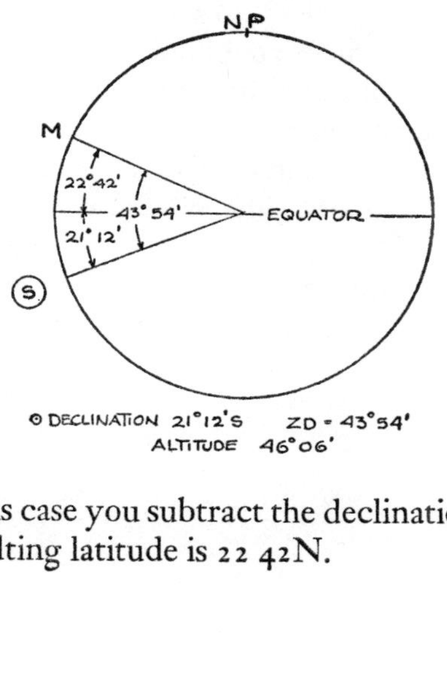

Obviously in this case you subtract the declination from the zenith distance. The resulting latitude is 22 42N.

When you are between the sun and the equator:

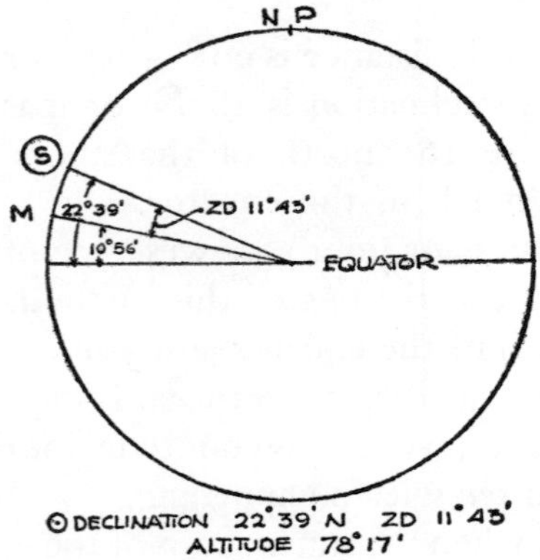

In this case you must subtract the zenith distance from the declination for the resulting latitude of 10 56N.

While the sun is the most commonly used body for latitude or meridian sights, the moon, stars, or planets can be used in this manner with equal ease or accuracy.

In all meridian sights the sextant is used in exactly the same manner as it is done in other sights. The same corrections are applied to change the Hs to the Ho.

To speed his work, the practiced navigator always sets down the zenith as 89°60′, rather than 90°, in determining the zenith distance.

WHEN we speak of *noon* in latitude sights we do not mean the kind of noon when the noon whistle blows. It is very rare that the two noons coincide, for, alas, the sun does not cross any meridian at the same time each day. If it did we wouldn't have to worry about time signals and life would be much easier for the astronomer as well as the navigator.

As it is impossible to make a watch that would follow the sun exactly each day, we set our navigation timepieces—as well as all the watches and clocks in the world—on the *average* time that the sun returns to the same meridian each day.

Therefore, the sun is sometimes ahead of our clock schedule and sometimes behind it, and to take our latitude sight we must use the almanac to find out exactly when the sun will be on our meridian.

This exact noon is known as *local apparent noon* (*LAN*); it may be as much as 45 minutes different from our watch time.

Determination of local apparent noon today, thanks again to the Air Almanac, is a very easy procedure. Once again we think in terms of GHA instead of longitude (remember that GHA is nothing more than west longitude), and turning to the sun's GHA column in the almanac, just reverse the process and read from right to left, or from GHA to GCT.

Let us take an example. Our dead-reckoning longitude is 71 27W and the navigation day is April 20, 1949. As west longitude is the same as GHA, we translate our longitude into GHA 71°27′. (If we were in east longitude we would subtract it from 360°.)

We turn to the daily page of the Air Almanac for April 20, 1949, and run down the GHA column of the sun (on the right-hand side this time) until we find the nearest interval below our own GHA.

15 00	45 16	N11 33	73 22	130 19	S20 12	281 12	N13 19
10	47 46		75 52	132 49		283 43	
20	50 16		78 23	135 19		286 13	
30	52 46	• •	80 53	137 50	• •	288 43	• •
40	55 16		83 23	140 20		291 14	
50	57 46		85 54	142 51		293 44	
16 00	60 16	N11 33	88 24	145 21	S20 12	296 15	N13 19
10	62 46		90 55	147 51		298 45	
20	65 17		93 25	150 22		301 15	
30	67 47	• •	95 56	152 52	• •	303 46	• •
40	70 17		98 26	155 22		306 16	
50	72 47		100 56	157 53		308 47	
17 00	75 17	N11 34	103 27	160 23	S20 12	311 17	N13 19
10	77 47		105 57	162 54		313 48	
20	80 17		108 28	165 24		316 18	

This turns out to be 70°17′ at GCT 16h 40m. That means that the sun will be on the meridian of 70 17W at 16h 40m. We now subtract 70°17′ from 71°27′ to find the distance away that meridian is from ours. That becomes 1° 10′.

Now we turn to the sun interpolation tables (you will find them reprinted on page 77), and working from right to left find how long it will take the sun to travel 1° 10′. This is 4 minutes and 39 seconds, which we add to the time of 16h 40m for a GCT of 16h 44m 39s.

Therefore, local apparent noon—the time the sun will be on our meridian and the time we should take our noon latitude sight—is 16h 44m 39s.

If you are very uncertain as to your dead-reckoning position or have no timepiece, you can still use the noon latitude sight in the manner it was taken before the chronometer was invented. This method is used even today by many coasters and fishermen.

Start shooting the sun well before LAN and continue taking sights for an indefinite period. As the sun approaches the meridian, the reading will continue to rise, then halt, then fall. Take your highest reading as the one when the sun was on the meridian, and proceed to work out the sight.

Almost any kind of an almanac (even the ones given away by patent-medicine concerns) will give you the sun's declination, and it is generally published in the weather column of daily newspapers.

Let us now do a noon latitude sight from start to finish. It is March 4, 1949, dead-reckoning position 20 26N, 61 37W, height of eye 12 feet, I.C. +3′. Hs 63° 01′. Sun bearing south. (Reprint of March 4 almanac pages will be found on pages 73 and 74.)

Determination of LAN

59 32W	=	16h 10m	GCT
2 05	=	8m 19s	
61 37W	=	16h 18m 19s	LAN

Sextant Correction

Hs	63° 01′
Dip	− 3′
I.C.	+ 3′
SD	+ 16′
Ho	63° 17′

Noon Latitude Sight

Zenith	89° 60′	(90°)
Ho	63° 17′	
ZD	26° 43′	
Declination	—6° 23S	
Latitude	20 20N	

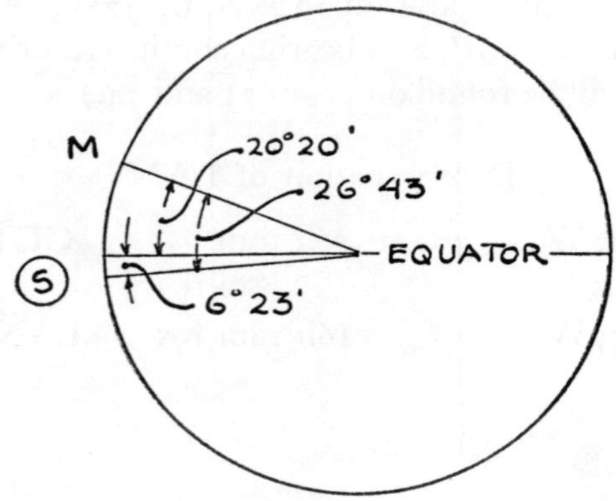

ELECTRONICS today plays as important a part in navigation as it does in ordinary life ashore. In many respects electronic navigation is easier and more accurate than dead reckoning or celestial navigation but it, too, has its weaknesses. There are many known errors and many unknown errors, commonly called "bugs," that haunt all forms of radio transmission and reception, and electronic navigation has its full share of both. In addition, a failure or sharp reduction in the power supply means the end of all electronic assistance.

Electronic navigation today can be divided into three major systems: *radio*, *loran*, and *radar*. In England two more methods have been developed—*consol* and *decca*—but they have not as yet won universal acceptance.

The simplest and most widely used system is radio bearings. Because of the low cost of the equipment and the ease of operation by unskilled hands, radio direction finding is very popular with yachtsmen, fishermen, and other small-boat operators cruising along the coast. Radio bearings are largely limited to coastwise navigation, as errors and difficulties of reception creep into long-distance signals.

The principle of the radio bearing is the same as that of the directional antenna and the factor of the portable radio that makes it play louder in one position than in another. As you will remember, a portable radio plays loudest when the enclosed antenna—generally in the back of the instrument—is parallel to the direction of the radio broadcast, and the signal disappears when the antenna is at right angles to it. The antenna of a radio direction finder is the same type except that it is free to revolve the whole 360° and its base is attached to a compass card.

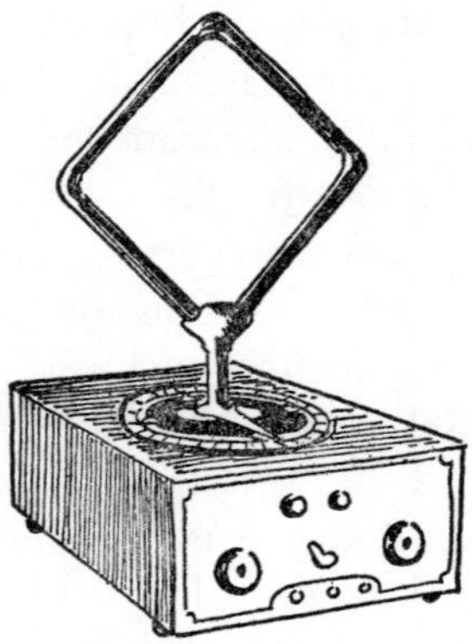

In operation the navigator puts on a pair of earphones, tunes in on a radio station, and turns the antenna until the signal disappears. He then reads the bearing on the compass card. As the direction finder is installed so that North is in line with the boat's bow, the reading is relative, and to make it true the boat's heading is added to it. The navigator then plots a line of position in the same manner he did when he took a bearing on a lighthouse.

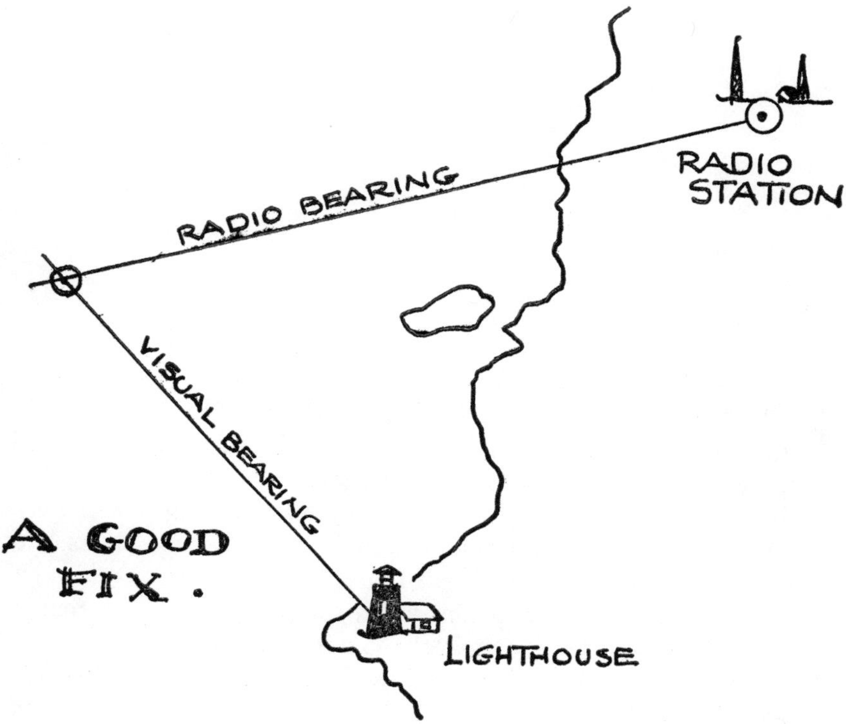

Sometimes the navigator uses regular broadcast stations; sometimes he uses aviation airway beacons; sometimes he uses government-operated radio bearing stations. The last are the safest, for, being transmitted from lighthouses, they are directly on the water and not subject to local interference. A map showing their location along the American coast will be found in the Light Lists published by the Coast Guard, or will be sent free from their headquarters in Washington. This map also gives the time and identifying signal of each station. On regular charts radio bearing stations are marked by a red circle, and the new coastwise charts will carry the location, signal, and frequency of standard broadcast stations and airway beacons.

LORAN and radar are war babies, but they have grown rapidly in peacetime. Because of the expense of the instruments and the power required to operate them, they are not generally found in small boats, although commercial fishermen are finding one or both instruments a profitable investment in locating fishing banks and home ports in fog and other times of poor visibility.

Loran is a very simple system based roughly on the fact that it takes a radio signal longer to travel 200 miles than 100 miles.

This principle in itself is not particularly astonishing and it was valueless until a device could be perfected that could keep up with the speed of radio waves—780,000 miles a second. A Loran receiver listens to two radio stations and tells which is the nearest and where to draw a line of position between them.

Naturally the unit of measurement is extremely small, and time as we know it is too clumsy. The Loran unit of measurement is the *microsecond.* This is one-millionth of a second and is to one second as a second is to 11½ days.

Loran transmitters, maintained by the governments of the United States, Canada, Great Britain, Denmark, and Iceland, are scattered over the two oceans in such positions as to give good cuts in lines of position. They are always in pairs—a master and a slave—generally several hundred miles apart.

In operation the master station transmits a signal—called a pulse—which is received and timed by the navigator's Loran set. This same pulse triggers the slave transmitter to send out a similar signal. Discounting the known time it took the signal to go from the master to the slave station, the Loran receiver tells the navigator how many microseconds longer it took one signal to reach it than the other.

Let us say a ship was in this position:

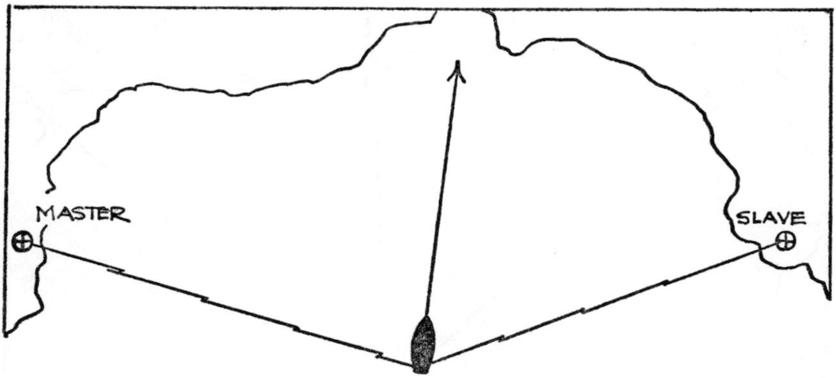

Obviously, here, the slave pulse will be received before the master pulse. The receiver cannot tell the distance off from either station but it can tell in microseconds the time difference between the arrival of the two pulses.

Now if you will look at this diagram below, you will see that no matter where the ship may be there is a definite connected series of positions where the time difference will always be the same.

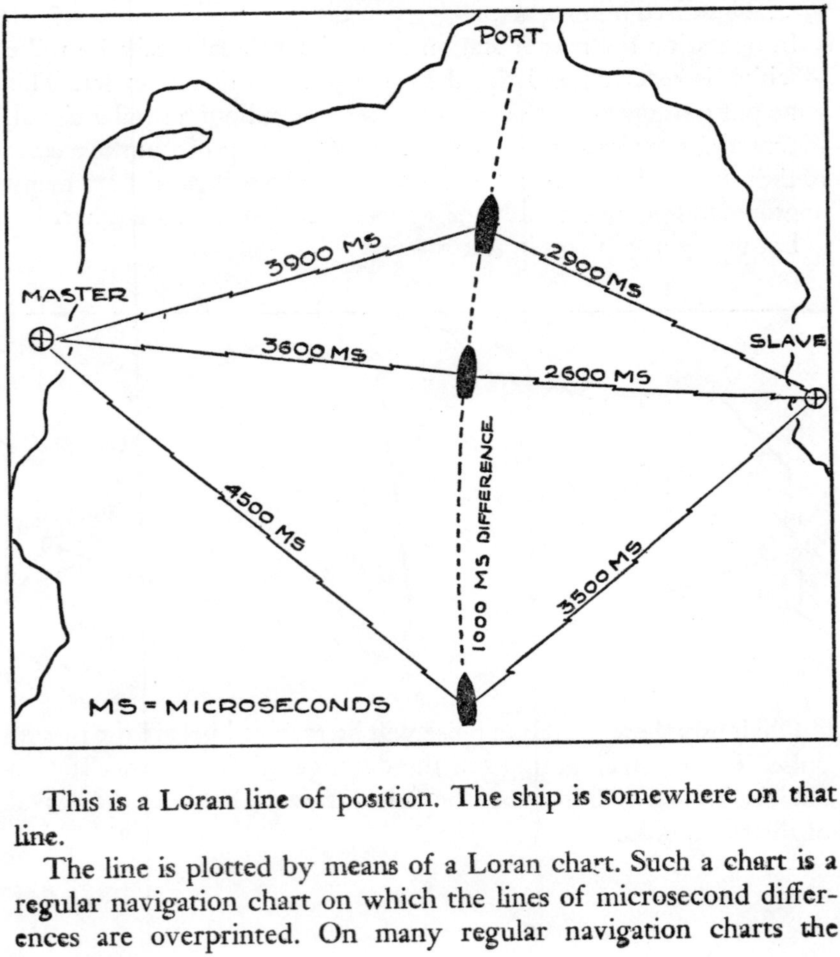

This is a Loran line of position. The ship is somewhere on that line.

The line is plotted by means of a Loran chart. Such a chart is a regular navigation chart on which the lines of microsecond differences are overprinted. On many regular navigation charts the

Loran grid is printed on the reverse side. A typical section of a Loran chart looks something like this:

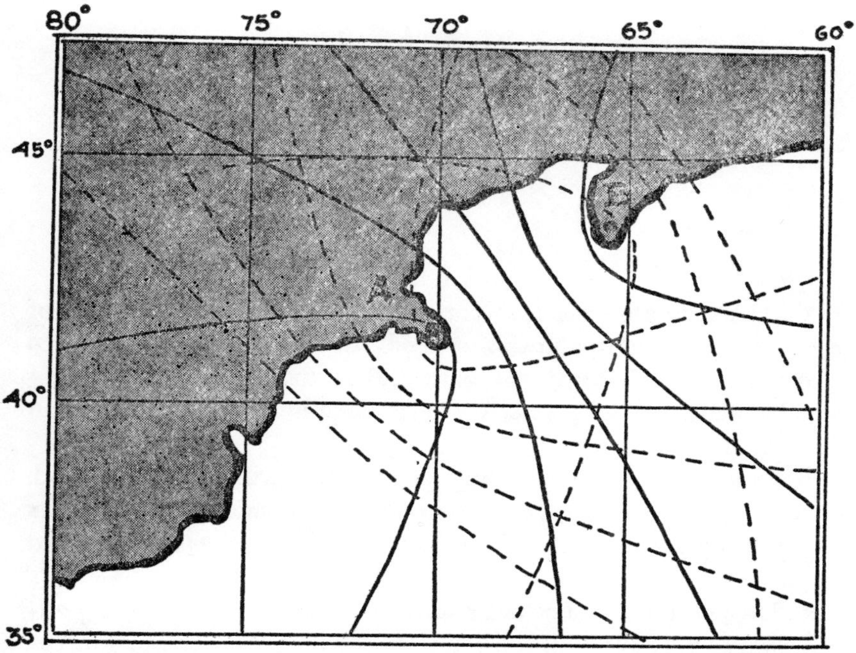

In practice, the navigator tunes in a pair of stations and determines their time difference. He plots the line with parallel rulers and dividers. Then he tunes in another pair of stations and repeats this process. This gives him two intersecting lines of position for a fix.

A Loran line can be crossed with any other line for a fix or advanced in the regular manner. Under ordinary conditions the Loran fix is the most accurate known in deepwater navigation.

RADAR, like Loran, is seldom found in small boats, because of its cost, weight, and power needs. But because of its ability to give the mariner eyes in the dark and in the fog, it is becoming popular with coastwise vessels where delay is costly. It is found in all large ships.

From a navigation standpoint radar is primarily a coastwise aid, for its range is limited by the horizon. Its deepwater value lies in its ability to detect other vessels and airplanes, as well as icebergs and derelicts.

Radar will show on a circular screen—called a *scope* or *plan position indicator* (*PPI*)—all solid objects above the water in all directions for the extent of its range. This reproduction appears as a vague silhouette, and correct reading of the scope calls for considerable practice.

The first appearance of an object will show as a persistent point of light, called a *blip*, which will enlarge and take shape as the vessel approaches it. While some objects never become recognizable to the untrained eye, experienced operators become quite expert in distinguishing between a rock and a buoy or a ship and an iceberg.

The principle of radar is very simple and is based on the discovery that certain radio waves will bounce back when they strike a solid object.

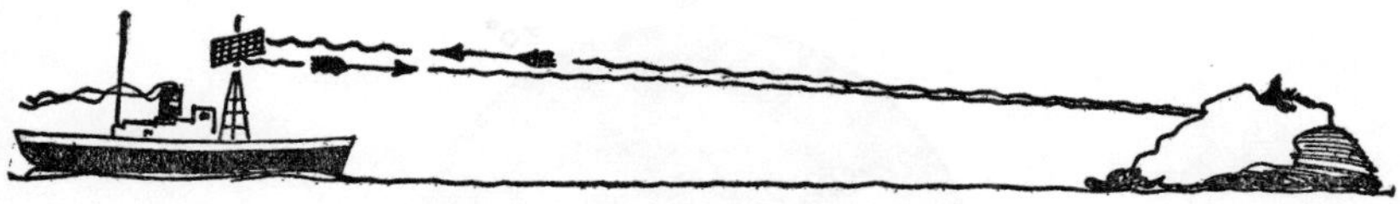

The radar set consists of a combined transmitter and receiver, both using the same antenna. A pulse is transmitted from the set, and if it strikes a solid object it will bounce back and be picked up by the receiver. As the pulse must be beamed—that is aimed in one direction like a gun—the antenna generally rotates slowly around a mast, transmitting several thousand times in each revolution.

(Here again we are working in microseconds, so that the transmitted signal and the return wave are so close together that for all practical purposes the mast has not moved in the meantime.)

On the PPI scope, generally mounted on the bridge, the object appears in its proper chartlike position as though we were looking down on the area from a point several miles directly above the radar set.

A small island 10 miles off might appear on the scope like this (the dot in the center is the position of the ship and 0° is the ship's heading):

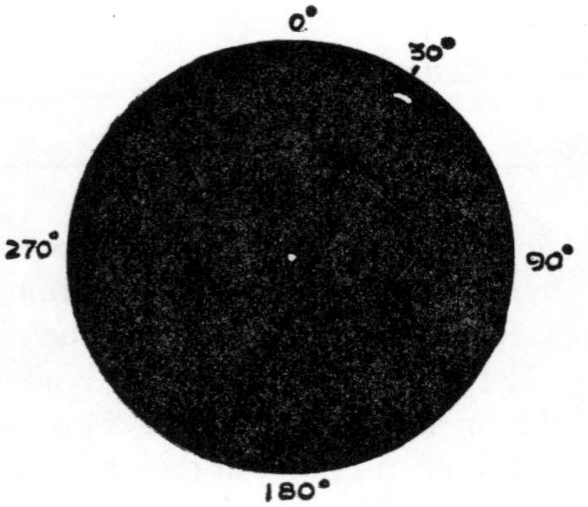

After 6 miles on the same course, the island would appear like this:

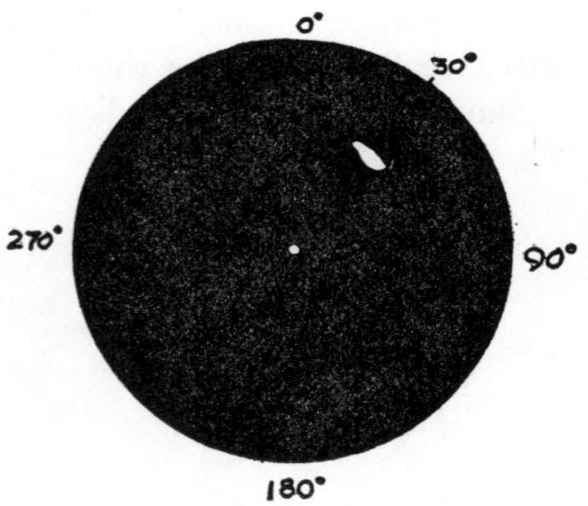

The scope is scaled so that the navigator can measure the distance off, and as a 360° compass rose encircles the scope he can determine the relative bearing of the island. Adding this to his heading, he can plot his position on the chart.

Naturally the higher the radar mast is installed the farther the receiver can see. At very high altitudes airborne radar sets will cover several hundred miles—scientists have even bounced radar signals off the moon—but naturally the longer the distance the poorer the visibility on the scope.

Marine radar sets generally have four or five shifts of range from 30 miles (possibly only with a very high mast) to as little as 1 mile, the range being shifted by a turn of a knob. This allows the mariner to follow an object from the time it is detected as a blip until it can be identified, for, naturally, the object is more and more defined as the range is decreased.

Navigation is only one phase of the value of radar. Its importance in preventing collision in fog or poor visibility is of inestimable value. As it is highly sensitive to approaching storms—a factor that was once regarded as a major "bug"—it is now extensively used in meteorology, permitting ocean liners to make safer and more comfortable crossings by detecting and skirting a storm area. It is used in search for survivors, in measuring wind direction and velocity, in locating schools of whale, and detecting drifting mines. In fact, not a week passes that another use is not found for radar.

An important development of radar is *racon*—the radar beacon. This is an electronic lighthouse that shows on the radar scope as a bright, coded signal in its true location, and enables the navigator to plot his exact position.

As yet the principle use of racon is in aviation, but more and more marine navigators are finding its value and the Coast Guard is now at work on a program to erect a network of racon marine beacons along the coasts.

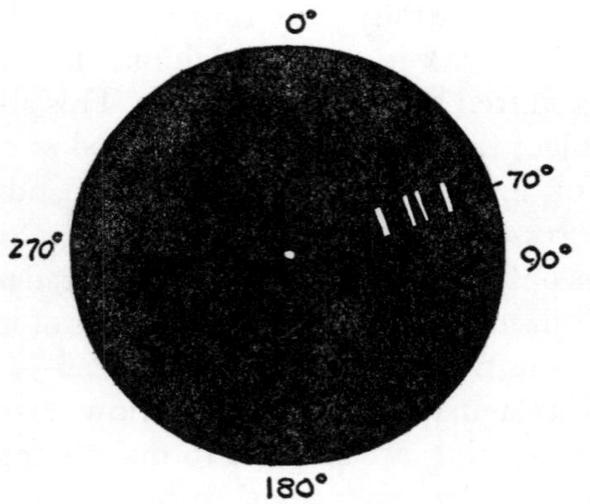

The above diagram is what a radar scope would look like if Rockaway Point racon beacon was bearing 70° relative from the receiver. The navigator would determine its distance off by measuring from the center of the scope to the center of the signal, thereby getting an absolute fix.

NOW having discussed the three families of navigation—piloting and dead reckoning, celestial, and electronic—let us see how a navigator puts them to use in a typical departure from an East Coast port.

This time we will presume that the navigator is on a ship leaving Boston for Lisbon, Portugal. To take advantage of tide and an uncrowded harbor, the departure is in the early morning. The pilot is dropped at Boston lightship and the navigator takes over the course of the vessel.

The date is March 4, 1949. The night is clear with frequent fog patches. Deviation 7° east on all courses. Variation 17° west. Height of eye 37 feet. Index Correction + 3′.

0310 Departure Boston lightship. Course 85° true, 95° compass. Speed 12 knots.

0405 Eastern Point light (Gloucester) bears 337° true.

0430 Thatcher Island light bears 338° true.
Radio bearing from Boston lightship 255° true.
Fix plotted at 42 24N, 70 26W.
Course changed to 80° true, 90° compass. Speed 12 knots.

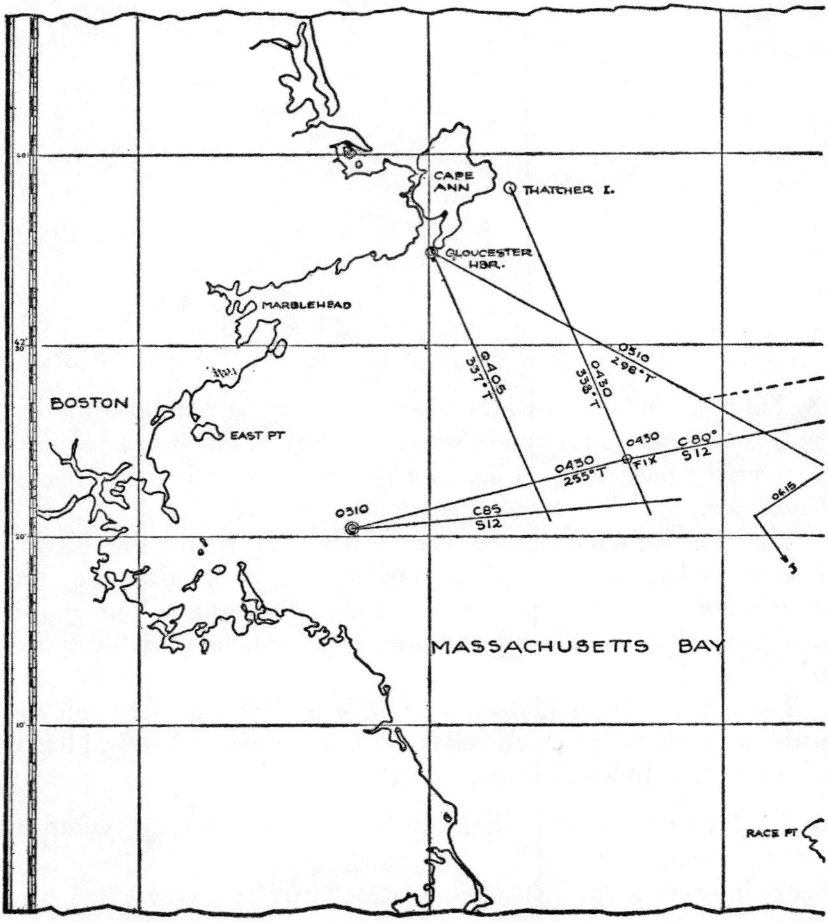
CAPE
ANN
THATCHER I.
GLOUCESTER
HBR.
MARBLEHEAD
BOSTON
EAST PT
0510
298°T
0405
337°T
0430
338°T
0430
FIX
C 80°
S12
0430
255°T
0310
C85
S12
0615
MASSACHUSETTS BAY
RACE PT

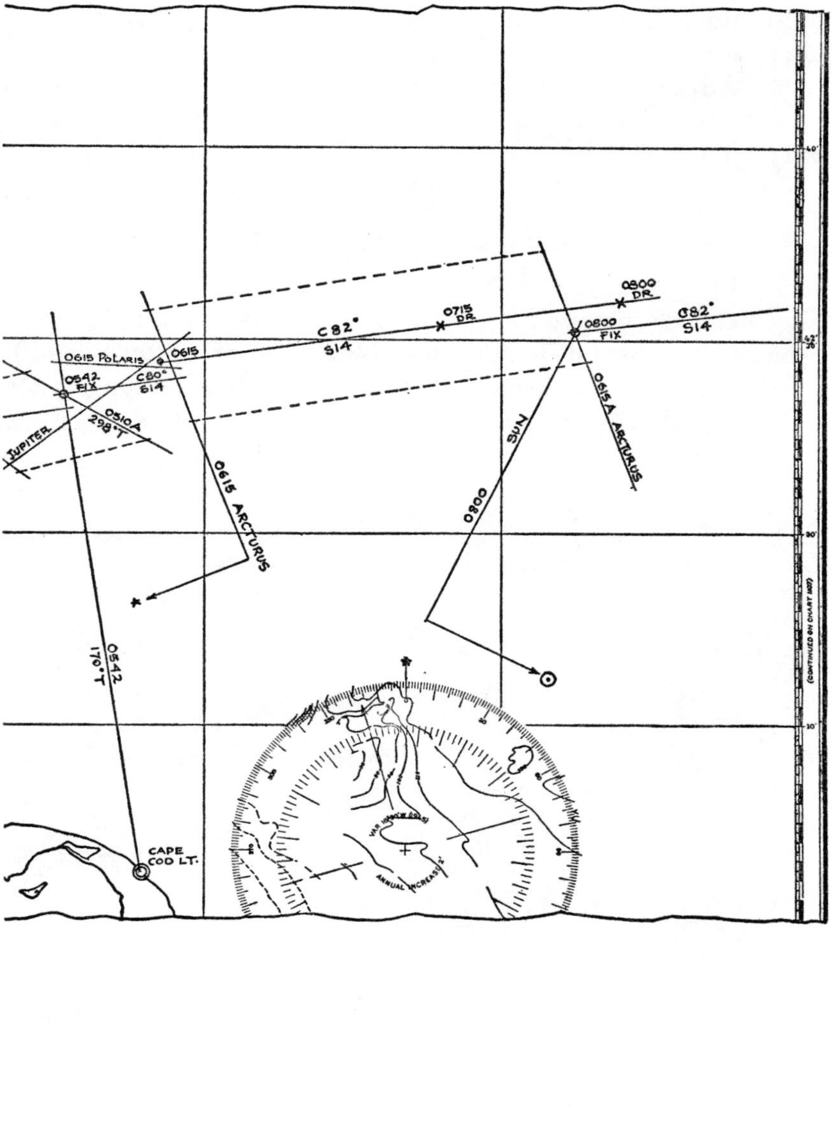
0800 DR.
0715 DR.
C82°
S14
0800 FIX
0615 POLARIS
0615
0542 FIX
C80°
S14
0510A
298°T
JUPITER
0615 ARCTURUS
0615A ARCTURUS
0800 SUN
0542
170°T
CAPE COD LT.
ANNUAL INCREASE 2'
40'
30'
20'
10'
(CONTINUED ON CHART 1107)

0510 Radio bearing from Eastern Point light 298° true.

0542 Radio bearing from Cape Cod light 170° true.
Advanced 0510 line for running fix. Position 42 27N, 70 09W. Course 80° true, 90° compass. Speed 14 knots.

0615 Three-star fix.

Jupiter	GCT 11h 01m 12s	Hs 17° 08.2′
Arcturus	11h 05m 19s	46° 03′
Polaris	11h 07m 46s	41° 56′

Fix plotted at 42 29N, 70 03W.
Course changed to 82° true, 92° compass. Speed 14 knots.

0800 Sun sight. GCT 12h 58m 42s. Hs 18° 08′ (Lower limb). 0615 Arcturus line advanced for running fix. Position 42 30N, 69 36W. Course 82° true, 92° compass. Speed 14 knots.

Jupiter

GCT	11h 01m 12s			Hs	17° 08.2′
GHA	30° 59′	Dec. 21° 26S		I.C.	+ 3′
Corr.	18′			Dip	— 6′
GHA	31° 17′			Ref.	— 4′
Ass. Long.	70° 17′	Ass. Lat. 42N		Ho	17° 01.2′
LHA	39°				
Alt.	17° 25.2′	d 87	Z 142°	Hc	17° 02.6′
Corr.	— 22.6′			Ho	17° 01.2′
Hc	17° 02.6′		Zn 142°	Int.	1.4′ Away

WORKSHEETS

Arcturus

GCT	11h 05m 19s		Hs	46° 03′	
GHA♈	326° 52′		I.C.	+ 3′	
SHA	146° 40′	Dec. 19° 27N	Dip	— 6′	
Corr.	1° 20′		Ref.	— 1′	
GHA	114° 52′ (474° 52′)		Ho	45° 59′	
Ass. Long.	69° 52′	Ass. Lat. 42N			
LHA	45°				
Alt.	45° 37.1′	d 66	Z 107°	Ho 45° 59.0′	
Corr.	+ 17.8′			Hc 45° 54.9′	
Hc	45° 54.9′		Zn 253°	Int. 4.1′	Toward

Polaris

GCT	11h 07m 46s	Hs	41° 56′
GHA♈	328°	I.C.	+ 3′
Ass. Long.	70°	Dip	— 6′
LHA♈	258°	Ref.	— 1′
Correction to Polaris + 37′		Ho	41° 52′
			+ 37′
		Lat.	42° 29′

Sun

GCT	12h 58m 42s			Hs	18° 08′	
GHA	9° 32′	Dec. 6° 27S		I.C.	+ 3′	
Corr.	2° 11′			Dip	— 6′	
GHA	11° 43′			Ref.	— 3′	
Ass. Long.	69° 43′	Ass. Lat. 42N		S.D.	+ 16′	
LHA	58°			Ho	18° 18′	
Alt.	18° 46′	d 75	Z 117°			
Corr.	— 20.3′					
Hc	18° 25.7′		Zn 117°	Hc	18° 25.7′	
				Ho	18° 18′	
				Int.	7.7′	Away

TIME DIAGRAMS

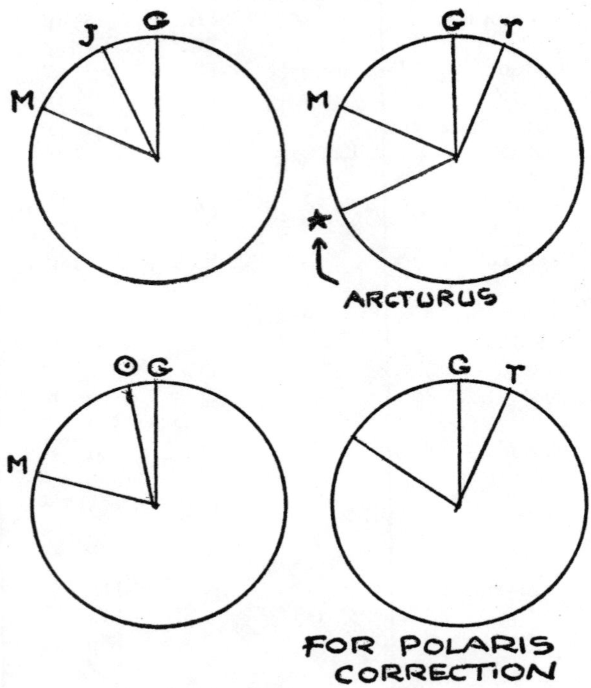

BIBLIOGRAPHY

For those who wish to continue the study of navigation the following books are recommended:

American Practical Navigator (Bowditch). The bible of American navigation. Tough going, but the final authority. Superintendent of Documents, Washington. $2.70.

Navigation and Nautical Astronomy (Dutton). The textbook for naval officers. Complete and up-to-date, but requires a knowledge of trigonometry. U.S. Naval Institute, Annapolis, Md. $4.00.

Primer of Navigation (Mixter). More comprehensive than the title implies. Very popular with yachtsmen and small-boat operators. Simply written and well illustrated. D. Van Nostrand, New York. $5.00.

Marine Navigation (Weems). A thorough and excellent book by a famous navigation authority. D. Van Nostrand, New York. $5.50.

Air Navigation (Weems). The pioneer book on this subject and still an outstanding work. McGraw-Hill, New York. $3.75.

Marine and Air Navigation (Stewart and Pierce). Covers a wide field but is unusually clear and expressive. Ginn and Co., New York. $5.50.

The Boatman's Manual (Lane). A handy, comprehensive book on seamanship and coastal navigation that is an excellent companion to this work. W. W. Norton, New York. $4.95.

GLOSSARY-INDEX

Dipper: The constellation *Ursus Major* which points to Polaris, the Pole Star. 93, 94

Dividers: 19–20

Doubling the Angle on the Bow: 12

Electronic Navigation: 103–114

Equator: A line around the earth, halfway between the poles, from which latitude is measured north and south. 33

Estimated Time of Arrival (ETA): 23

ETA: *See* above

Fix: A definite position or location, generally found by crossing two or more lines of position. 3–6

G: *See* Greenwich Meridian

GCT: *See* below

Greenwich Civil Time (GCT): The universal time of navigators, on which all navigation timepieces are set. Based on the time at Greenwich observatory in England. 46–49

GHA: *See* below

Greenwich Hour Angle (GHA): The distance, measured westward in degrees and minutes, of any celestial body from the Greenwich meridian. 49–51

Greenwich Meridian (G): The 0° meridian from which longitude is measured east or west, and Greenwich Hour Angle measured west. It cuts through Greenwich, a suburb of London. 34

Hc: *See* Computed Altitude

H.E.: *See* Dip

Ho: *See* Observed Altitude

H.O. 214: *See* Tables of Computed Altitude and Azimuth

Hs: *See* Sextant Altitude

Index Correction (I.C.): 68

Index Error (I.E.): A mechanical error of the sextant. 67–68

Intercept: The distance in minutes or miles of the line of position from the assumed position. 82

Knots: A vessel's speed in nautical miles per hour. 18

LAN: *See* Local Apparent Noon

Latitude: The distance in degrees and minutes of any position north or south of the equator. 31–35

LHA: *See* Local Hour Angle

Line of Position: A straight or gradually curved line plotted on a chart on which the navigator knows himself to be. 2–6

Local Apparent Noon: The instant the sun is on the observer's own meridian. 99–101

Local Hour Angle: The distance, measured in degrees and minutes, of any celestial body from the observer's own meridian. 52–56

Log, Navigation: The record kept by the navigator giving the hourly history of the voyage as to position, course, speed, etc.

Log, Taffrail: A device, similar to the mileage record of an automobile speedometer, to measure distance. 17

Longitude: The distance in degrees and minutes of any position east or west of the Greenwich meridian. 33–35

Loran: Long-range aid to navigation. 106–109

Lubber's Line: A hairline marking the bow line of the vessel on the inside of the compass bowl. 24

M: The local or the observer's own meridian. 52

Magnitude: The brightness of a star or planet. It is measured in reverse; the brightest star, Sirius is —1.6, while Polaris is 2.1

Mercator Chart: The most extensively used type of chart in navigation, on which all meridians of longitude are parallel and at right angles to parallels of latitude. 13

Meridian of Longitude: A line extending from the North to South Pole; the vertical line on a chart or map. 31–35

Microsecond: One millionth of a second. The time unit of Loran navigation. 106

Moon Sights: 86–87

Nautical Mile: The sea mile of 6080 feet, roughly one-seventh longer than the land mile. 16

Noon Latitude Sight: A sight on the sun taken when it is on the observer's meridian. 95

Noon Meridian Sight: *See* above

North Star: *See* Polaris

Observed Altitude (Ho): The altitude of a celestial body after it is corrected for errors. 71

Parallax: The error in moon sights caused by the distance between the observer and the center of the earth. 70–71

Parallel of Latitude: Any line north or south of the equator running parallel to it; the horizontal line on a chart or map. 31–35

Parallel Rulers: 19–20

Planets, Navigation: Venus, Jupiter, Mars, and Saturn, four members of our solar system. 86–87, 92

Planet Sights: 86–87
Plotting Sheets: Blank chartlike sheets to be used to plot course and position in deepwater navigation. 36–37
Polaris: The Pole or North Star, used extensively in determining latitude. 93–94
Pole Star: *See* above
Protractor: 6, 19, 21
Racon: The radar lighthouse or beacon system. 113–114
Radar: Radio detection and ranging. 110–114
Radio Direction Finding: 103–105
Radio Time Signals: 46
Range: Determining a line of position or a course by sighting two objects in line. 4
Refraction: The sextant error caused by the bending of light rays from a celestial body by the earth's atmosphere. 68, 69, 71
Revolutions Per Minute (RPM) Indicator: An instrument on power-driven vessels used in navigation to determine speed and distance. 17
Running Fix: A fix obtained by advancing a line of position to cross with another line of position. 9–10
Semi-Diameter: The sextant error in sun and moon sights caused by the breadth of the bodies. 69–71
Sextant: 42, 66–71
Sextant Altitude (Hs): The reading of the sextant before it is corrected for errors. 67
Sextant Errors and Corrections: 67–71
SHA: *See* below
Sidereal Hour Angle (SHA): The distance in degrees and minutes a star is west of Aries. 89–90
Speed and Distance: 16–18
Star Identification: 91–92
Star Sights: 88–90
Sumner Line: 65
Tables of Computed Altitude and Azimuth (H.O.214): A set of tables published by the Hydrographic Office for working out celestial sights. 79–80
Time: 45–51
True Course: The course plotted on the chart and uncorrected for variation and deviation.

Variation: The error caused by the difference in location of the magnetic pole and the true pole. 25–30

Vernal Equinox: *See* Aries

Z: *See* Azimuth

Zenith: The top of the sky directly above your head. 96

Zenith Distance: The distance from your zenith to the spot where the sun is directly overhead. 96

Zn: *See* Azimuth